Making Markets Work

Theme 4 for Edexcel A Level Economics B Year 2

Brian Ellis and **Nancy Wall**

Brian Ellis has been involved in teaching, examining, curriculum development, teacher training and writing. He sees it as important for people to think and to smile sometimes.

Nancy Wall was a teacher for 15 years. Since 1991 she has worked in curriculum development, with a particular interest in teaching strategies and classroom resource development. She is currently reviews editor of 'Teaching Business and Economics', the magazine of the Economics, Business and Enterprise Association. She has long experience of writing and editing resources for students.

Acknowledgements

We are very grateful for Paul Rapley's contribution to Chapter 12 and additional case studies, also to Karen Wilson for reading and commenting on several chapters.

Every effort has been made to trace the owners of copyright material, but in a very few cases this was not possible. We offer our apologies to any copyright owner whose rights may have been unwittingly infringed.

Anforme Ltd, Stocksfield Hall, Stocksfield, Northumberland NE43 7TN.

Typeset by George Wishart & Associates, Whitley Bay.
Printed by Potts Print (UK) Ltd.

Contents

Using this book

This book covers Theme 4 of the Economics B course. Most of the new content is best understood if you can link it to the ideas that figured in your earlier work in the subject. To help you revise, we have put reminders at the head of every chapter. They list the topics that are treated as prior knowledge required.

You are sometimes asked to draw a flow chart. Remember to identify every stage in the sequence of events. Don't leave anything out. When you are asked to draw a diagram, make sure it fits precisely the situation about which you are being asked.

Making links between different elements in the subject goes further than just revising the basic ideas that you have already encountered. To get a really good understanding of the content, you have to draw on aspects of the subject from many different topics, making connections between ideas and events. For example:

- The impact of macroeconomic policies must be studied against the backdrop of current trends in the labour market and in exports, imports and exchange rates.

- The behaviour of oligopolists in relation to pricing strategies requires a good understanding of demand elasticities.

To help you to draw on different areas of the subject we have included many cross-references that point you towards relevant details in other parts of this book.

This book is likely to go out of date rather quickly. Most readers will find there is much to learn about everything that has happened since the summer of 2016. We have included many issues relating to the UK's plan to leave the EU. But we do not know exactly how this is going to be accomplished. We can work out some of the likely medium–term consequences. But about the final outcome we know almost nothing at all. It is possible that these things will only become clear very slowly and after several years of negotiation.

There is another area of uncertainty, in that Europe has not yet fully recovered from the impact of the Financial Crisis of 2008-9. The UK and many other countries are still unwinding its consequences. Before all the necessary adjustments have taken place, new and perhaps unexpected events will begin to dominate the global economy.

So what should you do? Be very sure to keep up with events and changes as they occur – follow the news. Secondly, revise steadily all the time. Use this revision to help you to capture the links between different areas of the subject. It will actually enhance your understanding. The more you do this, the more often you will find that everything is falling into place. You should draw on different aspects of the subject to understand and analyse the effects of changes in policies, trends and events.

As you develop a deeper and more subtle understanding of economic problems you will begin to appreciate the massive complexities that surround us. It is only when you are really learning that you realise how little you know. Have courage. People who are well-informed are the cornerstone of global solutions. Being well informed means taking in the facts, identifying the range of perspectives that exist wherever there are difficult issues and drawing conclusions on the best evidence available.

Chapter 1

The spectrum of competition

Terms to revise: the price mechanism, substitutes, competition, consumer sovereignty, homogeneous and differentiated products, pricing strategies.

Vaping

The UK e-cigarette market grew rapidly, to about 2.6 million users by 2015. The share of smokers using e-cigarettes rose from 2.7% in 2010 to 17.6% in 2015 (ASH data). In the USA, the market at least doubled annually between 2010 and 2015, though growth has now slowed.

This is a controversial product, offering people dependant on nicotine an alternative with less damaging tars and toxins than cigarettes. The EU sees them as a tobacco product to be regulated and discouraged, but the Royal College of Physicians sees them as a valuable part of strategies to reduce tobacco smoking. Such contrasting views bring uncertainty and risk to suppliers. Also, major tobacco producers have entered the industry and offer powerful competition to small businesses.

A Researchandmarkets.com report suggests that global turnover in this industry will rise to $50 billion by 2025, creating space for both large and small businesses in manufacturing disposable and reusable e-cigarette systems and the consumable nicotine solution, in distribution and retailing, and also in e-cigarette cafes and clubs. This also implies some creative destruction via accelerated reduction in tobacco use and sales.

Discussion points

As the e-cigarette market grows, does competition become more or less intense?

Should governments regulate and discourage e-cigarettes in the same way as tobacco?

What attracts new entrants to an industry with such obvious risks?

Market structures

The extent and types of competition in markets vary widely. The **spectrum of competition** has examples of more or less competition. At one extreme there is **monopoly**, a situation where a sole supplier faces no direct competition. For example, many UK rail operator franchises give firms a monopoly on their routes or regions. One issue here is that although there is no direct competition, road travel is an available substitute in the broader travel market. This makes rail monopolies less powerful than others, such as water companies, where substitutes are less obvious. Assuming a normal demand curve, monopolists can choose either their price or the quantity sold.

Monopoly

A confusion to avoid is between monopoly and **monopoly power**. Firms have monopoly power if their market share is large enough for them to influence the market. The UK convention is to take a 25% market share as the threshold for monopoly power. This means that Tesco (28.4% of grocery sales in early 2016) and EE (32.9% of mobile phone services in 2015) have monopoly power but not monopolies. Both monopoly and monopoly power can be linked to high prices and profits.

Perfect competition

The opposite extreme to monopoly is **perfect competition**. This is a theoretical model which has attracted attention from economists for over two centuries. For analytical purposes, perfect competition has a string of assumptions: there are many firms which are each too small to influence market price or other firms, products are identical (or 'homogeneous'), there are no barriers to firms freely entering or leaving the industry and both buyers and sellers have perfect information (on products, output and prices). Although not often specified, the model also depends on there being many profit maximising entrepreneurs, all on the lookout for any chance to go beyond normal profits, in addition to rational consumers who consistently make the 'best' choices.

Normal profit

This combination would create intense competition. Prices would be competed down to the point where just **normal profit** is possible. Any business charging more than others would sell nothing, so firms become 'price takers', forced to accept the market price. Getting rich is virtually impossible as any innovation to cut costs or improve products will quickly be copied by everyone else (as they have perfect, i.e. full, information).

> The **spectrum of competition** is the range of levels of competition in supply to markets.
>
> **Monopoly** means there is a single firm which is the sole supplier to a market.
>
> Firms have **monopoly power** if their market share is large enough for them to have some influence over markets and rivals.
>
> The model of **perfect competition** uses strict assumptions to guarantee intense competition, which can be linked to efficient markets.
>
> **Normal profit** means just enough profit to keep firms in the industry, and is a key feature of the perfect competition model. Some theoretical analysis treats normal profit as part of costs.

The spectrum of competition

Figure 1: The traditional spectrum of competition

One firm	Two firms	Handful of firms	Many firms with differentiated products	Many firms with identical products
Monopoly	Duopoly	Oligopoly	Monopolistic competition	Perfect competition

Perfect competition theory

Demand is the result of utility (satisfaction) that products offer consumers. Each consumer is willing to pay up to the price justified by the utility of the product. Suppliers are forced to be cost efficient in order to make even normal profit and will supply at any price equal to their costs or above. The equilibrium quantity where demand and supply meet will be the point at which the cost of an extra unit just matches the utility it offers, which means that the ideal quantity of scarce resources are used for the product. The situation is summarised in the diagrams below:

Equilibrium

Figure 2: Perfect competition

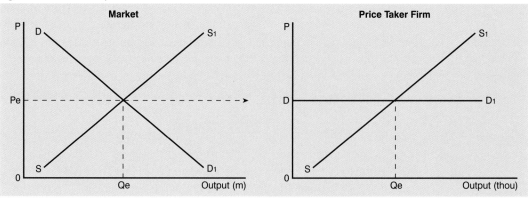

Should demand for the product increase, the market demand curve will shift up and right. This will increase price and send a positive signal to firms. Existing firms are likely to increase output and new firms might be attracted. As a result, market supply is likely to shift rightwards in time; so output and sales should increase again. This represents the market mechanism at its best, with price change signals leading to reallocation of resources, consumer sovereignty as their choices determine what is made, and efficient use of resources in order to stay in business.

> **Try this**
> Copy Figure 2 and then add to your diagram to show the sequence of changes triggered by a fall in demand for a product.

Perfect competition. An idealised competitive market will have all of the following characteristics:
- many buyers and sellers, each with too small a market share to influence price by their individual actions.
- identical (homogeneous) products from all suppliers.
- every supplier seeking to maximise profits.
- perfect knowledge of prices, technology and production methods.
- total freedom of entry and exit to and from the market.
- perfect mobility of factors of production.
- normal profit is inevitable in the long run.

Commodity markets

The attractions of this model mean that it is often treated as an ideal. Some markets are closer to this ideal than others, meeting most of its assumptions. Many commodities, for example, are identical or sold in homogeneous grades. Some commodities, such as coffee, have thousands of small producers. However, small growers at the start of the chain of production commonly live in isolated areas and sell to local dealers or traders; they have far from perfect information. At the retail end of the chain, businesses such as Nestlé have monopoly power in many markets.

Mining business BHP Billiton's revenue was $72 billion in 2012, and profits were $15.4 billion; such numbers do not suggest perfect competition in mining. Stock exchanges deal in homogeneous shares and other securities and there are many buyers and sellers. However, a limitation here is that a high proportion of trade is funnelled through leading banks and brokers, and the risks involved are estimated by just three ratings agencies. Scandals have revealed colluding traders using market power for their own gain. No individual market stands out as fully meeting the assumptions of perfect competition. However, the model illustrates how intense competition can bring attractive outcomes. As a generalisation, competition generally has better outcomes than monopoly power.

Imperfect competition

Any market between the extremes of perfect competition and monopoly is classed as imperfect. **Duopoly**, for example has two suppliers. **Oligopoly** has a few large firms, most often with additional small firms having very small market shares. For example, UK energy supply is dominated by six large oligopolists; a dozen smaller firms are trying to build from far lower market shares. (More on oligopoly in Chapter 3.)

Monopolistic competition

Early theorists thought that price competition would be the norm, but non-price competition has become increasingly important. **Monopolistic competition** acknowledges the importance of differentiation whilst keeping the other assumptions of perfect competition. Many real markets rely heavily on product differentiation; restaurants and clothing are obvious examples. Vaping suppliers are probably in this category now, but if the tobacco companies expand production, the industry may become more like an oligopoly with some smaller producers still competing.

Example

The hairdressing market consists predominantly of single salon operators. These can be differentiated in various ways. One US website suggests making the salon a 'client magnet' with a feeling of luxury and comfort. Salons can be trendy, or they can build a specialist reputation for classical style. They can target a market segment in terms of age or tastes. Some might compete on price, either consistently or by daily or weekly offers. This market has many features of monopolistic competition. Pub food in the local area is another example. Differentiating features might include large portions, Thai or French food, attractive décor, good locations, excellent beer or child-friendliness.

Duopoly exists in a market with just two suppliers.

Oligopolies have several dominant large firms, often also with smaller suppliers.

Monopolistic competition involves product differentiation but otherwise keeps the assumptions of perfect competition.

Pricing strategies

Competitive pricing

In highly competitive markets, where products are identical or very similar and there are many rival suppliers, competition makes the demand facing individual firms very price elastic. They have little alternative to competitive pricing. Whilst prices below average cost would be unsustainable in the long run, aiming for high profit margins would mean losing business to cheaper rivals. Firms will strive to cut costs and do what they can to attract consumers, but any source of competitive advantage is likely to be copied by other firms if it is effective.

With monopoly, the downward sloping industry demand curve is also the firm's demand curve. This means the firm can choose either the price to charge or the quantity to sell. Profit maximising monopolists will commonly charge a premium price and restrict output. This disadvantages consumers who must pay more than they would in a competitive market or do without the product.

Monopoly power

Where firms have monopoly power, they are still likely to face demand curves which slope downwards from left to right. This means that they will still sell less at a high price than a low one. The more price inelastic demand is, the more firms with monopoly power can profit from raising their prices. To maximise revenue (but not necessarily profit) firms should raise their price to the level where demand ceases to be price inelastic.

> **Think!**
> Why doesn't revenue maximisation always bring profit maximisation?

Price discrimination

In some case suppliers with market power can **price discriminate**, charging more to consumers with price inelastic demand and less to others whose demand is more price elastic. For example, rail operators charge more for rush hour travel when people need to get to work. Market power also opens possibilities for market skimming and penetration pricing to increase revenue. Alternatively, market power can allow predatory pricing to be used in an attempt to squeeze one or more rivals out of the market. If successful, this can increase a firm's control over the market.

> **Price discrimination** involves separating groups of consumers with different price elasticities of demand and charging higher prices to groups with lower PED.

> **Think!**
> When traders haggle with individual consumers, is this a form of price discrimination? Do students and young people sometimes benefit from lower prices because of price discrimination?

Non-price competition

Differentiated products

Many businesses see differentiation as a crucial element in their pursuit of profit. In monopolistic competition, for example, each firm seeks to give its product distinctive features (or unique selling points) which distinguish it from the opposition. If these features attract consumers, demand for the product will become less price elastic and profitability can increase. However, if we keep the assumption of perfect information, rivals can quickly copy successful features so profits are likely to fall back to the normal level. So, for example, the first cafés to offer free internet access drew in extra customers. Free internet access is now available in many cafés.

If we move further away from the competitive end of the spectrum, say to oligopoly, rivals are less able to match some forms of differentiation so the benefits can be longer lasting. Branding and marketing alone can be sufficient to differentiate a product. Gas retailers in the UK, for example, share a storage and distribution network. Each of them is required to put as much into the network as they sell, but there is a single standardised product. Market leader British Gas launched a 'Planet Home' marketing push in 2015 to build an emotional connection with consumers to reinforce its dominance. BG is now also paying more attention to its customer service, previously seen as weak.

Where sales are made online, speedy delivery is an attractive aspect of promotion. Next, for example, currently offers free next day delivery to a local store for orders placed before midnight. Next day delivery

How many of us can tell the difference between Coke and Pepsi?

at home (and same day delivery for orders before midday,) is available for a fairly low charge. Amazon 'Prime' customers have next day delivery as standard. Some firms see 'no quibble' guarantees and return policies as an attractive customer service feature.

Marketing

The most obvious source of differentiation is in the design, composition and performance of physical products; quality and reliability are important for both goods and services, in different ways. Customer service can be part of the differentiation package. Sometimes advertising, branding and other marketing strategies are more significant than product design. How many of us can tell the difference between Coke and Pepsi? Having brand names displayed prominently seems sufficient for effective differentiation in some cases.

Examples
Major car makers strive for a mix of power, fuel economy, safety, reliability, visual appeal and extra features to create an advantage over their rivals. Many electronic products engage in technological races; firms innovate frequently, attempting to get ahead and keep up. The subtleties with which clothing is differentiated can be difficult to keep up with.

Whatever route is taken to making a product distinctive, success will shift the brand away from the competition. As a result of this, price elasticity of demand should fall as rival products become less adequate substitutes. In turn, lower price elasticity will give the supplier greater control over pricing and profitability.

Perfect competition: limitations

Competition and efficiency

Though the model of perfect competition has features far removed from most reality, it does offer an attractive ideal. In a world of perfect competition, resources would be allocated efficiently, thanks to market signals. Powerful competition can force firms to keep costs low, creating productive (or cost) efficiency. (See productive and allocative efficiency, pages 24-25.) Where rivals compete on price, consumers pay less per item and are therefore likely to be better off.

Free market economists see the efficiency of markets as a sound reason to minimise the role of governments and regulation, which can distort outcomes by interfering with the market mechanism. Others suggest that real world market imperfections and failures are so widespread that extensive government control is necessary. There is a middle view here which allows a powerful role for market forces but favours intervention

Mixed economies

where it can correct market failures. This suggests that intervention can be beneficial, but also that too much control can create problems. Mixed economies combine free markets with a government role; the balance in the mix varies.

Real world complexities are such that any single move towards making markets freer and more competitive is not guaranteed to improve the situation.

Examples

Economies of scale may be impossible when there are many suppliers. And in the labour market, trade unions attempt to build some monopoly power, seen by some as a reason to ban unions. However, if major employers control a large part of demand in the market, banning unions might increase the imbalance in the market.

Exam style question

Skimming and penetration in the smartphone market

Global sales of smartphones totalled 1.4 billion in 2015. The largest market share and the largest increase in number of handsets sold went to Samsung (22% of all sales). Apple, with 16% of all sales, recorded a global record for profits. Huawei (7%), Lenovo (5%) and Xiaomi (4.5%) still have relatively small shares of the global market but their sales are growing at the fastest rate.

Apple focuses on design, innovation, a strong brand and its own operating system. This has made possible a variant on price skimming, with such frequent innovation that prices for the latest iPhone have never fallen before the next model is introduced. Samsung aims to produce the most advanced smartphones that use the Android operating system, sold at prices similar to Apple's. In addition, Samsung also markets less advanced mass market smartphones at lower prices, which help to explain its top market share. In 2015, for example, they introduced the J5 which sells at around £160, about a quarter of the price of top Samsung or Apple models.

With more than a billion potential consumers in each of their own countries, Chinese firms such as Huawei and Indian producers such as Micromax initially concentrated on their home markets. Most of their sales in Asia are of relatively cheap mass market models. In 2016 they widened their horizons and introduced more technically advanced products to become global competitors.

In spring 2016, Apple introduced the iPhone SE model. This has a smaller screen than the range topping iPhone 6 and sells at prices around 40% lower. This could be an example of market segmentation but could also indicate a readiness to compete more on price in future.

Questions

a) Using the data above, calculate the share of the smartphone market taken by the five largest suppliers *(4 marks)*

b) Explain where the smartphone market fits in the spectrum of competition. *(4 marks)*

c) Explain how Samsung can have the largest increase in handset sales yet Chinese suppliers have a faster rate of growth. *(4 marks)*

d) Analyse two advantages which could have helped leading Chinese suppliers to increase their sales rapidly. *(6 marks)*

e) Discuss the sources of market power held by Samsung and Apple. *(8 marks)*

f) Assess the case for the Chinese manufacturers using penetration pricing when launching their most advanced smartphones in North American and European markets. *(10 marks)*

g) Evaluate the case for Apple to introduce more price competitive smartphones. *(12 marks)*

h) Evaluate the consequences of oligopoly for smartphone consumers. *(12 marks)*

Chapter 2

Barriers to entry

Terms to revise: product differentiation, branding, internal and external economies of scale.

Patents

Patents

A patent gives its owner the right to stop others making, selling or using an invention for a period of up to 20 years. The purpose of the patent system is to encourage innovation and technological progress. For example, Alexander Graham Bell was granted a patent for the telephone in 1876. The Bell telephone company later became AT&T and is currently one of the 25 largest companies globally. Firms supplying goods with a unique selling point will often patent the distinctive feature of their product to prevent others copying it.

Patents have a major role in the development of new medicines. Patents for drugs to help cure life threatening diseases are extremely valuable, with some patented treatments priced at more than $250,000 per patient per year. The pharmaceutical firms justify this by saying that development can take 15 years and costs are above $2 billion per successfully patented drug, but inelastic demand for effective cures and legal monopoly power help to explain the price charged.

Discussion points

How do patents encourage technological progress?

Does the monopoly power created by patents work in the interests of consumers?

How ethical are the very high prices of the most expensive medicines?

Contestability

There are some markets in which low start-up costs and limited regulation make it easy to start a business. For example, offering unwanted items on eBay provides a simple and cheap introduction to selling for anyone with access to the internet. On a bigger scale, despite start-up costs, regulations to be followed and a high failure rate, there is no shortage of people ready to start restaurants and other food outlets. If starting a business is easy, the market is **contestable**.

Barriers to entry

> A **contestable market** is one which firms can enter and leave easily. One general feature of such markets is that sunk costs are likely to be low.
>
> **Sunk costs** cannot be recovered once incurred. Machinery and premises can be resold, but marketing costs (for example) cannot be recovered by a firm leaving the market, so they are lost or 'sunk'. Such costs are a barrier to entry and to exit as they are irretrievable and increase risk.

We can identify a set of theoretical conditions which would provide 'perfect' contestability:

Figure 1: Perfect contestability

No barriers to entry or exit	No sunk costs	Free access to technology and resources	No natural monopoly

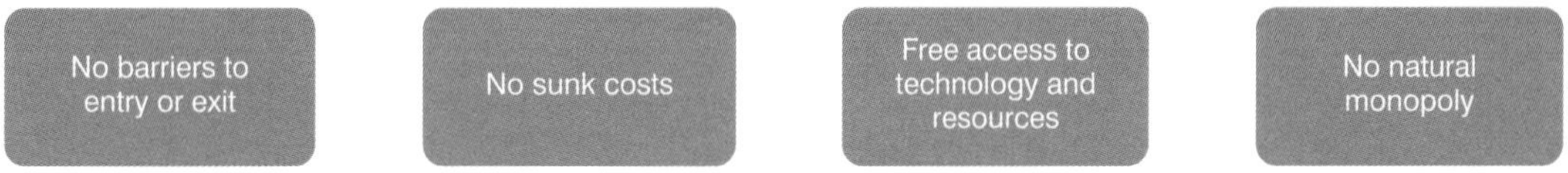

Contestability was identified as a significant factor in markets by William Baumol, over 30 years ago. He argued that contestable markets could stop firms from exploiting monopoly power. High profits would attract new entrants, increasing industry supply and so forcing down prices and profits. Even 'hit and run' entrants, just in the short run, could profit from entering a contestable market if prices were high. A monopolist knowing this should keep prices down to avoid attracting rivals. The central idea here is that contestability can work like current competition to protect consumers from monopoly power.

The Competition and Markets Authority (CMA) and industry regulators such as OFGEM value contestability. They will act to reduce barriers to entry where they can, to keep prices down for consumers. Firms with monopoly power, on the other hand, can sometimes construct barriers to reduce the chance of new competitors taking market share and forcing prices down.

> **Barriers to entry** are obstacles making it harder for new firms to enter a market. High barriers to entry reduce competition and can allow existing firms to exploit monopoly power. Barriers can be legal (e.g. **patents**), natural (e.g. internal economies of scale) or artificial (caused by existing firms).
>
> **Patents** give inventors the right to be the only producer of their new product for a period of years. New processes can also be patented.

Show your understanding

1. Hairdressing is a contestable market. Identify three more.

2. Now identify three markets that are definitely not contestable and explain why.

3. Explain why patents make sense, even though they reduce competition and raise prices.

Legal barriers to entry

Patent infringement

Where a firm has patents for products or processes, rivals who copy them risk expensive legal action. For example, in the 'smartphone patent war' a court in California awarded Apple $1 billion compensation from Samsung for patent infringement, though this award was subsequently reduced. Tobacco and alcohol are subject to heavy regulation in many countries (see page 59). Governments commonly keep a public sector monopoly over defence and elements of the justice system and may prohibit or regulate production and distribution of some products such as guns and recreational drugs.

Regulation

A court in California awarded Apple prodigious compensation from Samsung for patent infringement.

There is protection for **intellectual property rights**. Besides giving creative artists and performers exclusive rights over their work (called 'copyright'), this extends to brand names and symbols. One of the ways in which subsidiaries transfer revenue to parent firms is via licence fees for the use of branding and symbols. Stealing protected ideas is treated in the same way as patent infringement.

Intellectual property rights

> **Intellectual property rights** protect the creations of peoples' minds. This is an umbrella term including copyright for writers and musicians, patents for inventors and trade secrets for firms.

Regulations aimed at protecting consumers provide another legal barrier. Only qualified 'gas safe' fitters are allowed to install new gas boilers. Dental qualifications are necessary for filling or extracting teeth. Without qualified staff, it is impossible to operate businesses in such areas.

Natural barriers to entry

Natural monopolies

A **natural monopoly** exists where duplication (e.g. of railway lines between cities or of water supply pipework infrastructure) would be expensive, impractical and perhaps also wasteful. Sometimes internal economies of scale are so extensive that there is little room for competition. Average cost reduction from economies of scale for the existing firm(s) might put any new entrant at such a disadvantage that they would have little prospect of matching the lower cost and price at which their larger rival(s) can operate. Such economies can be linked to necessary research, capital equipment, raw materials, production, distribution or marketing. When large scale is necessary to achieve low costs, high start-up costs are enough to deter many potential competitors.

Example

Royal Mail plc lost its monopoly of postal deliveries in 2006. Some rivals carry letters in bulk between cities but use Royal Mail for 'the last mile' of delivery from sorting offices. Dutch owned 'Whistl' tried to compete for full 'end to end' letter services but pulled out of the market in mid-2015. A falling volume of letters makes it harder for any newcomer to match Royal Mail's economies of scale. For parcels, a growing market has sufficient volume for multiple firms to compete.

In many areas of manufacturing, a new supplier needs to invest heavily in physical capital such as machinery and premises before starting operations. Funding high start-up costs can be extremely difficult for an unproven business, brings extensive risk and may be very expensive. Where existing firms have economies of scale, this problem is compounded: starting small would be an added disadvantage. This barrier is even greater if a high proportion of start-up costs are sunk costs.

A **natural monopoly** is an industry where costs will be higher with multi-firm supply than with a sole supplier. This often results from heavy infrastructure or distribution costs.

Internal economies of scale

External economies can help new entrants as much as existing firms, whereas internal economies give a cost advantage to established businesses. Lower costs allow them to be profitable at prices below the unit cost of smaller entrants. This makes it difficult for a newcomer to compete with large existing firms. The table below gives a recap on the main internal economies.

Economy	Description	Example
Technical	Costs rise less than productive ability as size increases. Equipment can be used more fully.	A container that doubles capacity needs less than double the materials. e.g. specialist tyre changing equipment.
Marketing	Larger scale spreads fixed costs of advertising and promotion across more units.	Multinationals can use material such as TV advert visuals in many markets.
Risk bearing	Firms with many products or markets can cross-subsidise losses in one area.	Pharmaceuticals, diversified conglomerates.
Managerial	Small firm entrepreneurs take on many tasks; expert specialisation is possible in large firms.	Specialists in human resources, research, logistics and accountancy can be more effective.
Purchasing	Bulk-buying allows larger firms to negotiate better terms.	Monopsony power. Supermarket chains can 'squeeze' smaller suppliers.
Financial	Lower borrowing costs as large firms are perceived to be less risky.	Easier availability and lower interest rates on bank loans.

Artificial barrier: product differentiation

Products with distinctive qualities can stand out in the minds of consumers. To get noticed and compete effectively, rivals might need to more than match the qualities, performance or reliability of an existing product. Consumers might only be attracted if a new variation surpasses their established choice in a significant way. This might require extensive and expensive research and testing, with no guarantee that the added feature will appeal to sufficient consumers. Alternatively, if differentiation is based on marketing and image, any newcomer will need to accept the extensive sunk costs of building an image.

Artificial barrier: branding

Brand loyalty

A brand name can be sufficient to establish a strongly differentiated image and a clear preference. People commonly 'Hoover' the floor or 'Google' an internet search. There are alternatives, but many consumers have brand loyalty which has become habitual. Even where products are standardised, as in the case of petrol, many buyers stick to a 'preferred' brand. Although a brand image is strongly associated with the product, it can be developed almost as a separate entity, perhaps with an emotional hook to reinforce loyalty. Loyalty schemes such as Nectar and Clubcard can strengthen branding further.

Advertising

Artificial barrier: spreading risks in R&D and new technologies

Pharmaceutical firms suggest that research and development costs around $2 billion per successful drug treatment; this is a high risk business. The largest firms in the market are Novartis and Pfizer, each with annual revenue above $40 billion. The revenues of 11 pharmaceutical companies exceed $20 billion p.a. each. A significant share of this revenue is ploughed back into research and development for new treatments. Such large firms spread risk by running multiple research projects, accepting that some are likely to end in failure. An entrepreneur from outside this market is unlikely to take the risk of starting up

Pharmaceutical firms suggest that research and development costs around $2 billion per successful drug treatment.

in competition with them. Research scientists with a potential breakthrough are likely to see the dominant firms as most capable of taking their work forward, so many new ideas are channelled through the giant firms.

Spreading risks

In the market for expensive perfumes, leading firms each produce a range of brands and accept that some new perfumes will fail. Any newcomer would have a greater chance of failure because of the strength and brand proliferation of the established firms. Internet giants such as Alphabet (Google), Apple and Microsoft can run multiple lines of research into possible new technologies and also take over small firms which have promising projects, anticipating that some profitable breakthroughs will cross-subsidise failures elsewhere. Small firms don't have the resources to spread risks in this way.

> **Try this**
> Active Google projects in 2015 included Google Glass (mainly for business use), Google Fibre, Android Wear (smart watches), Android Auto (driverless cars), SpaceX (mainly satellite use). Identify two other potential developments that may succeed.

Artificial barrier: vertical integration

Vertical integration can bring power over supply chain inputs or retail markets. When producers own retail outlets, they can make life difficult for independent retailers or rival producers. The six large UK energy suppliers are vertically integrated from generation and wholesaling to retailing. Small new energy retailers have a very weak bargaining position when buying gas or electricity from any of the large six firms. When Vodafone and EE stopped supplying it with handsets in 2014, Phones 4U went out of business.

Market power

Even without integration, large firms can negotiate exclusive contracts with suppliers or retailers, blocking other firms from access to supplies or to the market. For example, car makers commonly give dealers exclusive rights to a geographical area. This is an effective barrier to entry within the defined area.

Artificial barrier: predatory and limit pricing

If existing firms are known for aggressive pricing policies, potential entrants can be deterred. Predatory pricing occurs when a large firm deliberately sets its price below cost, intending to drive one or more competitors out of business. This requires financial reserves or other products which can cross-subsidise losses in the short run. In the long run the predator hopes for monopoly power and high profits. In 2013, Esso and Shell were accused of localised predatory pricing by independent filling stations. Retail prices charged by the two giants, where independents were allegedly targeted, were lower than the wholesale price of fuel. Further back in time, News International sold 'The Times' newspaper at 10p on Mondays to draw customers from rivals such as 'the Daily Telegraph' and 'The Independent' (which has since gone out of business).

Regulators such as The CMA can act against predatory pricing (see pages 13-14). It is clearly anti-competitive. However, cases are hard to prove and rivals can be damaged before effective action is taken. Limit pricing is more subtle. Price is set low enough to deter new entrants but not at unprofitable levels. Deciding precisely where to set a limit price depends on anticipating the costs of newcomers so might not be precise. Lower prices can be used temporarily when there is the possibility of new entrants, or permanently if a firm settles for lower long run profits in order to retain its market power.

A perceived threat of predatory or limit pricing acts as a barrier to entry if potential entrants fear they will be unable to make profit as existing firms might force prices too low for them to survive.

The impact of barriers to entry on market structure

Legal, natural and artificial barriers to entry shift reality away from the perfect competition assumption of easy entry and exit. The extensive range of real world barriers is one reason why markets are frequently near the less competitive end of the spectrum of competition.

Natural monopolies

In the case of natural monopolies, having more than one supplier entails wasteful duplication and so poor use of resources. At the same time, a monopolist has market power and the potential to exploit consumers. Potential profits can be very high where demand is price inelastic, as in the case of domestic water supplies, for example. Some governments keep natural monopolies in the public sector and operate them 'in the public interest'. A danger in this approach is that there will be no competitive pressure on such monopolies to operate efficiently so they could suffer from the problem of **X-inefficiency**. At the extreme, they could even be more wasteful than competing firms would be.

> **X-inefficiency** is a waste of resources which occurs when a firm has little incentive to control costs. This is often due to lack of competition. Low PED can contribute to X-inefficiency as it allows higher costs to be passed on via higher prices.

Privatisation

A wave of privatisations in many countries from the 1980s transferred many natural monopolies to private ownership, with competition introduced where practical. Regulators limit exploitation by privatised monopolies with pricing controls and other powers. The effectiveness of regulators is open to debate but their existence can restrict abuse of power. (More on this in Chapter 7.)

Examples
For UK electricity, National Grid has a monopoly of the distribution network, with competition in generation and retailing. BT retains a monopoly of the fixed line telephone network in most of Britain but there is competition in its use. Water companies have monopolies in their regions.

Global oligopolies

Consumer markets often have both economies of scale and artificial barriers such as branding. In many cases this has resulted in oligopoly. Globalisation has created some global oligopolies. A limited number of large firms dominate such markets, though smaller firms can often co-exist with the major ones. The ability of oligopolists to exploit market power and make high profits depends on the nature of competition in the market. There is often an emphasis on non-price competition. Product differentiation effectively reduces the price elasticity of demand for branded items so producers gain market power. (See Chapter 3.)

Intermediate markets for parts and services supplied to businesses often involve standard specifications so branding and differentiation are less significant. These markets are often more price competitive though barriers to entry can still exist. In the case of computer central processing units (CPUs), for example, differentiation and extensive R&D have built an 80% market share for Intel. AMD have more than 10%; barriers to entry for new firms are significant.

Labour intensive primary product markets, e.g. for cocoa, coffee, cotton, flower growing and rice, are often highly competitive. But even in agriculture, mechanisation and automation can create economies of scale which bring a cost advantage to giant producers (of wheat, for example). Agricultural markets are also often regulated and protected, so market forces and potential gains from competition can be restricted.

Exam style question (Section C)

Using information from this chapter, evaluate the extent to which barriers to entry help to explain the global oligopoly in sports shoes.

(20 marks)

Chapter 3

Oligopoly

Terms to revise: competitive advantage, market shares, pricing strategies.

UK Retail Banking

The Competition and Markets Authority (CMA) is investigating the retail banking market in the UK after finding that current account services and lending to small businesses "lack effective competition". Customers are given limited information. Market leader Lloyds has almost 30% of the market (CMA data), even after being forced to transfer 631 branches to TSB. Barclays, RBS, HSBC and Santander average around 15% each, so all other banks have just 12% of the market between them.

Challenger banks (such as Metro Bank, TSB and Virgin Money) are comparatively small. Three big obstacles to their growth are cost disadvantages due to economies of scale, the complexities of secure computer system requirements in this market and the extent of consumer inertia.

Discussion points

What problems could result from "a lack of effective competition"?

What might explain consumer inertia in this market?

Is the growth of online banking likely to lead to increased competition?

Concentration ratios

Market shares

The quickest way to identify an oligopoly is to add the market shares of the large firms in the industry. There is no set number of large firms – this varies from industry to industry, though the normal range is from three to seven. Market share can be measured by revenue or by quantity of items sold; revenue is used more often. When the large firms have more than half of the total market this indicates oligopoly. If they have 100% there are no small firms in the market.

> **Concentration ratios** measure the market shares of large firms in an industry. A limited number of large firms having more than 50% of the market is seen as an indicator of oligopoly.

Try this

Use the data in the case study above to estimate the 5 firm concentration ratio in UK retail banking. (There are two possible answers because the percentages are approximate.)

A pure monopolist will be one firm with 100% of the market. In perfect competition even a 10 firm concentration ratio would show a tiny market share. In many cases, the largest firm in an oligopoly will also have some monopoly power, indicated by a market share above 25%. Lloyds bank is one example of this. Market share and concentration ratio data is most often used in oligopoly situations.

Interdependence and price stability

A key feature of oligopoly is that the market shares of the large firms are big enough for the actions of each of them to have an impact on the market and their rivals. Thus, for example, if one major supermarket chain starts a price war, the others are likely to respond. When Phones 4U closed, this gave a boost to other major mobile handset retailers. In other words, oligopolists are interdependent. Their market shares and their profits will be influenced by what their rivals do.

Price wars

Price wars are rarely in the interest of oligopolists as they are likely to damage revenue and profits for all the major firms. Price competition is possible if one firm believes it has a cost advantage or believes that

Predatory pricing

predatory action can remove a rival and so bring long term gains. However, oligopolists are wary of cutting prices when it might well lead to retaliation and lower profits for everyone. Price cuts are more likely to be used as a short term tactic to increase market share. If market share gains can be sustained, this is likely to increase potential long-term profits. Often oligopolists will not want to risk a price war. So stable prices may become the norm for long periods.

> **Interdependence** refers to the way oligopolies will each take decisions in the light of the actions or expected reactions of competing businesses in the industry.
>
> **Price wars** involve a series of competing price cuts which are likely to lead to losses for some firms in the industry. They may be started by a dominant firm with a predatory pricing strategy.

Each firm needs to consider the implications of any initiative rivals take, also to take account of rivals' likely reactions to their own tactics and strategies. This doesn't mean that they don't compete, but it helps to explain the emphasis on non-price competition. Firms try to outwit each other to win market share and profits.

Figure 1: Examples of market concentration

Market concentration

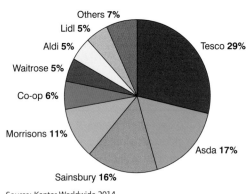

UK supermarket market share, 2014

Others 7%
Lidl 5%
Aldi 5%
Waitrose 5%
Co-op 6%
Morrisons 11%
Sainsbury 16%
Asda 17%
Tesco 29%

Source: Kantar Worldwide 2014

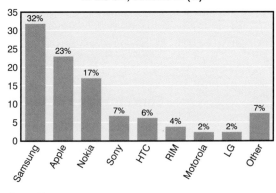

Market share of mobile handset manufacturers in the UK, June 2014 (%)

Samsung 32%, Apple 23%, Nokia 17%, Sony 7%, HTC 6%, RIM 4%, Motorola 2%, LG 2%, Other 7%

Source: Company reports

Try this

How many large firms would you include for concentration ratios in the two markets above?

Use web research to see how market shares have changed from the 2014 data shown.

How might firms have competed in order to increase their market shares?

Using the information in the case study (page 13), discuss the extent to which banks compete.

Competition

Oligopolists tend to rely heavily on seeking competitive advantage through non-price competition. This can be intense, with heavy expenditure on research, innovation and marketing. Unique new features are

Non-price competition

defended strongly; this can be via legal action. Firms appear to strive relentlessly for any source of advantage over rivals. Reactions to anything rivals do is rapid and as forceful as possible. Car producers have extensive economies of scale, so work hard to maximise sales of each model. Markets for many electronic products have intense non-price competition, stressing technical features.

If large firms use differentiation, build brand loyalty, research product improvements and innovate, this can both give an advantage over existing rivals and erect an entry barrier to discourage new entrants. It is no accident that products from toothpaste to trainers and yogurt to yachts will all try to do these things. Success for one firm will spur rivals to respond.

By contrast, some oligopolies appear relatively calm. Prices tend to be stable if individual firms see price increases as risky to market share and lower prices as risky to profits because of probable retaliation.

Market stability

Marketing maintains existing brand loyalty with only limited customer movement between brands. Innovations seem relatively minor. This description might fit the market for household cleaning products, which is dominated by Unilever and Reckitt Benckisser. Both individual features and prices are fairly stable. Attempts to increase market share are visible mainly in their advertising and promotion, sometimes with occasional technical improvements.

Figure 2: Price and non-price competition

Tacit collusion

If large firms collude and act together, it becomes possible for them to share some monopoly power. They can avoid competing and behave like a monopoly. For example, they might all be able to charge higher prices at the expense of consumers. This is illegal but firms may each independently find their way to a realisation that strenuous competition could harm them all. They can behave as if there were colluding, but without ever contacting each other. This is **tacit collusion**, sometimes referred to as tacit agreement.

Collaboration

> **Example**
> If we accept that the six leading UK Energy suppliers have no hidden agreement, they perhaps illustrate the potential for tacit collusion. They have each independently found the benefits of splitting operations into generation, trading and retail businesses. They all blend standing with variable charges in different ways, making clear price comparisons difficult. They all seem to change prices in the same direction (more often upwards) within a short period of time. On paper, their retail arms just make respectable profits but their trading businesses seem to make the big profits.

Price leadership

Tacit collusion often involves **price leadership**. One firm, not always the biggest, makes decisions on price changes. Others follow, either to the same level or to restore differentials between brands to the previous levels. When one petrol filling station in a particular locality changes its price, for example, others in the same area will often quickly follow. Such quick reactions to price cuts can stem from intense competition, with rivals striving to maintain their market share. However, if they follow price increases just as quickly this shows that market share is not always given priority.

Tacit collusion comes to an end if a price war develops. As price wars usually mean lower profits for most competitors, very often all parties will strive to avoid starting a price war. Stability is safer. They may compete on value for money – perhaps by differentiating the product and charging premium prices for high quality or fashionable products. Other forms of non-price competition will be very important too. It is easy to see why market stability might be preferable to constant price warfare.

Where firms quite openly reach an agreement, perhaps even with a contract, there is **overt collusion**. Competition law in many countries bans collusion in order to protect consumers. The simple truth is that collusion is likely to result in higher prices for customers. Sometimes overt collusion is allowed if it is 'in the public interest', e.g. when an important transport link might otherwise close down.

Overt collusion

Example

The UK competition authorities are generally in favour of multi-operator ticketing agreements where more than one bus operator serves an area. Allowing passengers onto any bus regardless of which firm's ticket they have bought makes life simpler and can shorten travelling times, so encourages more use of bus services. This is an approved form of overt collusion.

It seems probable that the retail banks in the case study on page 13 are not guilty of overt collusion, but clearly there is consumer inertia. This makes it very easy for them to avoid competing and make little effort to reduce their charges or improve customer service.

Tacit collusion involves firms separately coming to understand that it is in their joint interests not to compete vigorously, without any contact or agreement between them.

Price leadership often forms part of tacit collusion, with one firm making price changes that others quickly follow

Overt collusion means firms openly agreeing to action which is in their joint interest. This is anti-competitive and generally illegal.

Price discrimination

Figure 3: Consumer surplus

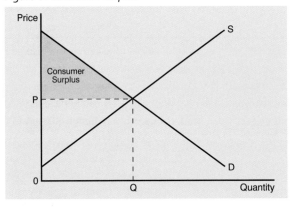

Most economic theory uses assumptions which lead to a single price in a market, yet in reality there are many situations in which prices for the same product vary. The best starting point in explaining this is the demand curve. We draw a demand curve assuming, quite reasonably, that products have a stronger appeal to some consumers than to others. Top left on a demand curve are those who value a product most and are willing and able to pay most for it. The market price is likely to be below the amount they are willing to pay so they have consumer surplus. In a sense, they get a bargain because they would be willing to pay more.

Price discrimination involves firms charging different prices to different consumers for the same product, essentially to capture some consumer surplus. This is only feasible if three conditions apply:

● There must be barriers to entry, or rivals will undercut the higher price.

Differing price elasticities

● Different groups of consumers must have differing price elasticities of demand and be willing to pay different amounts.

● Groups of consumers must be easily distinguishable, to prevent 'leakage' of consumers between groups or traders buying at the lower price and reselling to those with less price elastic demand.

Example

Price discrimination works for peak and off-peak rail travel. Rush hour travellers often need to travel to work on time so their demand is price inelastic. Leisure travellers have more price elastic demand. A standard class 'anytime' return from Bath to London, for example, is currently £185, whilst an off-peak return is £71.20. That ignores the possibilities of railcards and advance booking, which can be seen as other forms of price discrimination (young people and senior citizens might have lower incomes so be more price sensitive). Higher first class prices are NOT price discrimination as the product is different (more leg room and comfort, maybe free tea and coffee).

Businesses which have the right conditions can use price discrimination to increase their revenue. Consumers who pay the lower price gain benefit from a product they might not otherwise have had. Paying the higher price is a disadvantage, so, for example, some commuters resent the ability of other types of traveller to pay off-peak fares. However, railway lines would struggle to be profitable just on the basis of peak business during the limited time of rush hours. Any additional revenue at other times might help to keep lines open.

Haggling

The extreme ('first degree') form of price discrimination is a situation where each consumer is charged a different price, according to what they are willing to pay. Some haggling market traders and antiques businesses try to get as close to this as they can. With no marked prices, their initial price quote is often high. They might then slowly reduce their price as they try to work out the maximum that the customer is willing to pay.

Customer loyalty or inertia

Customer loyalty was thought to win consumers better service from firms which valued their repeat business. Recently, though, there has been a trend to take loyalty as a sign of inertia and so of low price elasticity of demand. Consequently, businesses such as some insurance companies, utility suppliers and subscription television services have price discriminated by charging loyal customers more. Lower prices are offered to new customers and to those existing customers who show readiness to take their business elsewhere. Even where there are set prices, customers willing to haggle can sometimes talk their way to paying less.

Exam style question (Paper 3)

Discrimination
(Use the evidence below and ideas from this chapter.)

United Airlines had 43 different prices for economy tickets for flights between Los Angeles and Chicago, varying from $109 to $1765. If they could have filled planes at $1765 per ticket they would happily have done so, but only a few customers are willing to pay that. Limited numbers of seats were allocated to lower price levels. Cheaper prices also brought more conditions (such as non-refundable fares, booking well ahead and flying at relatively unpopular times). The main point of these conditions is to put off  those customers who are willing to pay more. A complex computerised 'yield management' system is used in an attempt to maximise the total revenue from each price.

Questions
a) Discuss reasons why the air travel market is oligopolistic for flights between many
   airports. *(8 marks)*

b) Assess the price elasticity of demand for air travel. *(10 marks)*

c) Assess the conditions necessary for price discrimination in air travel. *(12 marks)*

d) Evaluate the consequences of United Airlines price discrimination for passengers
   and for the airline. *(20 marks)*

Chapter 4

Business objectives and pricing decisions

Terms to revise: average costs, revenue and profit, minimum efficient scale, price elasticity of demand, contribution, business objectives, pricing strategies.

Growing strawberries

Bill Thomson has a sheep farm close to the South Downs in Sussex. But he has used some of his land to grow high quality strawberries which he sells through local farm shops. He can sell all he can produce but only if he charges a price not too much higher than that of other small-scale growers. Over the season his price averages £7 per kilo.

His fixed costs are quite low; rent for the land works out at about £2,000 a year. Variable costs – planting, cultivating, picking and delivering amounts to about £4 per kilo. Last year he produced 650 kilos. His variable costs include the cost of his own time.

The table below has columns for quantity produced (Q), variable cost (VC), fixed cost (FC), total cost (TC), marginal cost (MC), total revenue (P x Q) and profit. Fill in all the columns (except the MC one).

Q in Kgs	VC (4 x Q)	FC	TC (VC+FC)	MC	TR (P x Q)	Profit (TR-TC)
600		2000				
650						
700						
750						
800						
850						

1. How will Bill be feeling at the end of the year and why?

2. He reckons he can easily produce more with the land that he has, probably up to 800 kilos. Explain why this may be a good idea.

Marginal cost

Marginal cost is the extra cost of producing more. Now work out what each extra batch of 50 kilos will cost – this is the addition to total cost. Marginal revenue is the amount that each additional 50 kilos will bring in. As long as Bill can expand output, his sales revenue will rise by that amount every time he grows an extra 50 kilos.

Average cost, average revenue and profit

Average cost is the total (fixed + variable) costs divided by the quantity produced. Average revenue is total revenue divided by quantity sold and will be the selling price if just one price is charged.

$$\text{Average cost} = \frac{\text{Total cost}}{\text{Quantity sold}} \qquad \text{Average revenue} = \frac{\text{Total revenue}}{\text{Quantity sold}}$$

Profit

Profit is the amount by which total revenue is greater than total costs. The bigger the surplus of average revenue over average cost, the greater the profit on any output will be.

Fixed costs	Costs which don't vary with output in the short run, such as rent
Variable costs	Costs that change directly with output, such as materials used
Total cost	The sum of all fixed and variable costs per time period
Total revenue	The sum of revenue received (often price x quantity) per period
Average revenue	Revenue per unit sold. TR/Q. Normally equal to price
Total profit	Surplus of total revenue over total costs
Profit per unit	Average revenue minus average cost

Show your understanding

Calculate Bill's average cost, average revenue and profit if he grows 750 kilos of strawberries. Do you think Bill ought to raise his selling price? What might his best strategy be?

By definition, businesses will make profit at output levels where average revenue is above average cost. Under perfect competition, producers can sell all they can produce at the going market price. Bill is in a situation quite close to perfect competition, but because his strawberries are particularly good, he can charge just a little more than the going rate for a kilo of strawberries from other growers. So he does make a bit of profit above a certain level of output.

Average total costs and economies of scale

Operating efficiently at minimum average costs helps profitability. Economies of scale explain why the long run average cost curve of firms tends to slope downwards as output increases from low levels. The realistic shape of the long run average cost curve will vary from industry to industry. Few economies are available in some cases and a natural monopoly might never reach diseconomies of scale. However, in price competitive industries it is important to reach the size at which average cost is minimised. This size is called the minimum efficient scale. Firms below this size will have a cost disadvantage. Firms encountering diseconomies as output increases will see average costs rising.

Minimum efficient scale

Figure 1: Long run average costs – minimum efficient scale

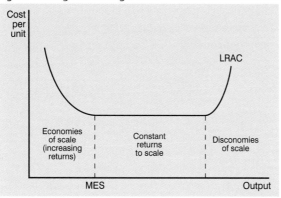

Minimum efficient scale is the lowest level of output at which average cost is minimised.

A tidy theoretical picture doesn't necessarily match reality. Where there are global oligopolies, extremely large firms stay competitive despite any diseconomies. Either they find ways to counteract diseconomies or they successfully differentiate so consumers will pay more for their brands. Diseconomies might set in

Most businesses, when working out how much to produce, will be thinking about a little more or a little less output.

very quickly where flexibility and speedy communication are needed, so minimum average cost can be at low output levels. Figure 1 suggests that a wide range of outputs have minimum average cost, but sometimes there could be just one least cost output level. Theoretically, this could lead to firms in the industry all being of very similar size.

The safest generalisation is that where competition is based on price, there is an advantage for firms of a size where average costs are minimised. They can charge lower prices than rivals or have bigger profit margins (profit per unit). Small firms such as start-up businesses and large firms with diseconomies will be at a disadvantage.

Marginal cost and marginal revenue

Profit maximising output

Marginal cost and marginal revenue can be used to determine the profit maximising output for a business. Most businesses, when they are working out how much to produce, will be thinking about a little more or a little less output. The effect on costs and revenue of producing more or less will determine how much profit they will make. Even though most entrepreneurs don't understand the marginal principle, they will be well able to estimate the impact of changing output.

> **Marginal revenue (MR)** = the change in total revenue from selling one more unit of output.
>
> **Marginal cost (MC)** = the change in total costs from making one more unit of output.

Marginal cost and marginal revenue focus on small changes in costs and revenues from increasing or decreasing output by just one unit. If making and selling one more unit adds more to revenue than it does to costs (MR > MC), then this will be worthwhile. If the last unit made adds more to costs than to revenue (MC > MR), reducing output will increase profits. Logically, profit will be maximised at the output where

MC = MR

MC = MR.

Under perfect competition marginal revenue and average revenue and price are all equal – because the business has no control over the market price and there will be no profit over and above the amount needed to stay in business. Its demand curve will be horizontal. It can sell all it can produce at the going market price – if it charges more it will sell nothing and if it charges less, it will make a loss.

Marginal revenue	Things will be different for a business that has an element of monopoly power: it will have a downward sloping demand curve. Take, for example, a monopolist who could sell 10 units at a price of £10 (TR = 10 x 10 = £100) but would have to reduce price to £9.50 in order to sell 11. 11 x £9.50 = £104.50. The MR of an 11th unit is £4.50 whereas price is £9.50. This means that its demand curve will slope downwards. Part of the money received for the 11th unit is balanced out by having to accept a lower price (50p less) for the previous 10.

> **Calculate** Bill's marginal revenue when he increases output by 50 kilos. Explain how he might maximise his profits. Would this be a practical target for him?

Deciding on price and quantity

Continued price cuts with a downward sloping demand curve will eventually lead to a fall in total revenue and negative marginal revenue. PED will vary as we move along a straight line demand curve, the top end will have more price elastic demand and elasticity will decrease as quantity increases. Once demand is price inelastic, marginal revenue will be negative.

Try this

Price (£)	10	9	8	7	6	5	4	3	2	1
Demand	1	2	3	4	5	6	7	8	9	10

Calculate PED for price cuts from (1) £10 to £9 and (2) £2 to £1.

At what price(s) is there maximum total revenue?

Would a profit maximiser ever charge a price below £6?

Why is a revenue maximising price not necessarily a profit maximising price?

In the example above, a change in price from £6 to £5 brings no change in total revenue, so marginal revenue is 0. This is an indicator of maximum total revenue, but not of profit maximisation unless there are no marginal costs. If the marginal cost in this example is £3 per unit, the 4th unit has MR of £4 (£28-24) and so is profitable. A 5th unit would bring MR of £2 (£30-28), which is less than the £3 marginal cost, so selling a 5th unit would not be profitable. If MR exactly equalled MC at any output, we take that as the profit maximising output, even though the marginal unit would add the same amount to costs as to revenue.

Marginal cost is more straightforward. Given the premises, equipment and other fixed costs, moving up from very low levels of output might bring greater efficiency and so less added costs for an extra unit. Fixed costs are spread across the increased output. But if output increases further, MC may rise if the business encounters bottlenecks, congestion and overtime payments. These are short-term diseconomies of scale; they will reduce efficiency. At this point producing extra units will push up marginal cost.

Marginal cost, marginal revenue and contribution

Covering fixed costs	MC and MR analysis allows us to identify the profit maximising output. Contribution is defined as the amount each sale raises towards covering fixed costs or making profits. Extra costs from one extra unit of output (= MC) are likely to be variable costs. (Fixed costs don't vary with output in the short run.) As long as MR is above MC, an extra sale will make a contribution towards fixed costs or profits.

The contribution approach can also be used where markets are separated and/or there is price discrimination. It is unlikely that many off-peak rail travellers pay more than the average cost of a journey, because fixed railway costs are high. However, an extra passenger adds negligibly to fuel costs for a train and the biggest additional cost might be for a paper ticket. Marginal cost is very low so off-peak travellers make a contribution towards fixed costs or profit. Similar analysis can be applied to other forms of transport, to cinema and other entertainment, and wherever there is a set capacity in terms of customer numbers.

Try this

Brompton bikes have a distinctive small wheel design and fold to a convenient size. They are made in Brentford (London) in a relatively labour intensive way. Output has increased during this century from 6,000 to around 40,000 per year, with rapid export growth. New bikes sell at prices from around £1,000. Profit in the last financial year was £3.5m, around 13% of turnover. This suggests that average cost is around £850 (ignoring retailer margins).

Should Brompton accept an order from a new export customer offering £600 each for 500 bikes? What additional information would help to inform this decision?

Marginal cost and contribution

The triangle on the left shows how revenue from a sale might be split up. Marginal cost would be the variable costs of an extra unit. The area of fixed costs plus the area shown as profits can be seen as the contribution from the sale.

The impact of objectives on pricing strategies

Ups and downs at Sports Direct

Sports Direct started from a Maidenhead store, selling mainly stock bought cheaply from Asia. Expansion was rapid, e.g. by taking over small rivals. Early stores were often in basements or upper floors with lower rents, but this has changed. A large Lilywhites store in Piccadilly Circus was added in 2002. Acquisitions have now included sports goods brands such as Dunlop, Slazenger, Donnay, Karrimor and Lonsdale. Several brands were bought when close to bankruptcy. Hundreds of stores now sell discounted leading brands such as Adidas and Nike, plus cheaper brands owned by Sports Direct. The company became a plc and the share price reached a peak of 800p in August 2015. Annual sales in 2015 were £2.7 billion.

Profit vs. reputation

The business strategy has four key components: identifying brand acquisitions and property, investing in stores and employees, developing the website and online sales and promoting group-owned brands. The giant main warehouse at Shirebrook (Derbyshire) quickly ships stock to stores and overseas. Early 2016 brought problems. One description (Yahoo) said the business was famous for 'cheap t-shirts, big profits and zero hours'. Use of zero hour contracts and the working conditions in Shirebrook and stores have been criticised. Claimed price cuts have been seen as misleading by some. It has been suggested that heavy discounting causes 'brand erosion' in consumer perception in the long run. The company issued a profits warning. The share price fell by more than 50%.

1. Where does Sports Direct stand on the spectrum of competition?
2. How might a business such as Sports Direct benefit from buying brand names from struggling firms?
3. Does heavy discounting have disadvantages as well as advantages?
4. What objectives does Sports Direct appear to prioritise?

Business objectives vary. Some are concerned with survival; some are primarily focused on growth and profitability.

Growth
Profit maximising
Sales maximising
Market share

Survival
Satisficing
Social objectives
Employee welfare

Reputation
Customer satisfaction
Cost efficiency

Some firms have no choice; they must price competitively. To survive, they are forced to charge the market price and to sell all they can at that price (see Chapter 1). This can be a very good way to make a living but not, on its own, bring great riches.

Pricing strategies

Going for growth involves building market share by charging low prices in the short run, so that demand increases. Prices must be high enough to cover costs but low enough to attract customers in large numbers. This is penetration pricing – one aspect of the Sports Direct model. Once market share is significant there may be a degree of monopoly power that opens up pricing options and potential for greater profit. Premium pricing may be appropriate for high-end products. Skimming the market with new products or variants may be possible. Differentiation may permit a range of pricing strategies.

USPs

Better brand loyalty will increase demand and reduce PED. Focusing on differentiation and marketing might take short run priority over profits. The business will be better able to thrive whatever competition it faces, because it will have USPs that provide some monopoly power. Just striving to design a better product creates a competitive advantage. Focusing on specific market segments, tailoring the product to their needs may increase profitability.

Social objectives

Ethical priorities, **social objectives** and concern for employee welfare can in fact be consistent with growth and profitability. Of course these businesses must cover all of their costs if they are to survive. But a social enterprise or a charity offering something useful might achieve significantly more than the profit maximising output and be very successful. Reputation may actually attract customers

Exam style question

The Theatre Royal

The Theatre Royal in Bath first opened in 1805. Like many theatres, its finances are stretched. In its lifetime it has had prosperous periods and come close to closure more than once. Turnover in the year to mid-2015 was £13.5m and there are 150 employees. The charity which now runs the theatre prioritises its continued existence rather than profits, but needs to break even to survive. There are now more leisure substitutes for theatre going than ever before. For example, in recent years cinemas have begun showing relayed live theatre performances from top venues.

The main Theatre Royal auditorium has 900 seats. Research and experience suggest it can sell 800 tickets for a forthcoming performance at £30, revenue will be £24,000. To fill the theatre it believes that the price must be dropped to £25.

Questions

a) Explain the likely marginal cost if an additional customer (the 801st) attends a theatre performance. *(4 marks)*

b) Calculate the effect on revenue of charging £25 rather than £30 per seat. *(4 marks)*

c) Explain what the revenue change in (b) implies about price elasticity of demand. *(4 marks)*

d) Analyse the effect of more substitutes being available on demand for theatre tickets. *(6 marks)*

e) Discuss the potential for a theatre to price discriminate. *(8 marks)*

f) Assess the possible impact of revenue from programme, ice cream and bar sales on a choice between higher and lower ticket prices. *(10 marks)*

g) Assess the relevance of the concept of 'contribution' to theatre ticket pricing. *(10 marks)*

h) Assess the likely impact of charitable status on a theatre's objectives and pricing. *(12 marks)*

Chapter 5

Productive and allocative efficiency

Terms to revise: productivity, product and process innovation, opportunity costs and trade-offs, market orientation.

UK productivity and income

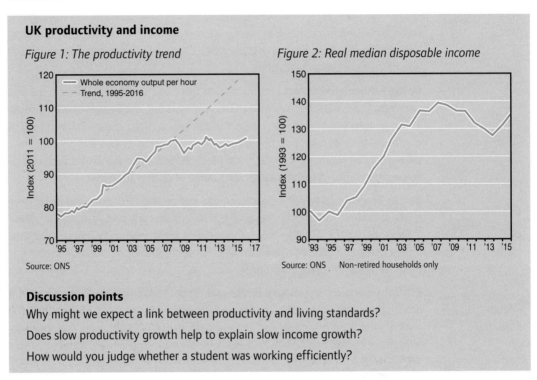

Figure 1: The productivity trend

Figure 2: Real median disposable income

Source: ONS

Source: ONS   Non-retired households only

Discussion points

Why might we expect a link between productivity and living standards?

Does slow productivity growth help to explain slow income growth?

How would you judge whether a student was working efficiently?

The distinction between allocative and productive efficiency

Efficiency

Resources are scarce and have an opportunity cost, so how we use them matters. Efficiency has two dimensions to an economist. If we are making the best choices about what to produce that is **allocative efficiency**. **Productive efficiency** is concerned with minimising the resources used and so the cost of making whatever goods and services are chosen. For a student, productive efficiency might include developing skills as much as possible in the time available, whereas allocative efficiency would be concerned with studying what will be most useful.

> **Allocative efficiency** means producing the goods and services that maximise satisfaction and match the preferences of consumers.
>
> **Productive efficiency** involves minimising cost (and avoiding waste) to produce as much as possible from the available resources.

Profit signalling mechanism

Free markets can help to generate allocative efficiency, guided by the 'invisible hand' of market forces. If a change in tastes creates more demand for a product, price is likely to rise. A higher price acts as a signal to firms that profits are available. If the revenue available is more than the costs involved, firms will enter the market and increase supply. Output should increase to the point where the marginal benefit to consumers is equal to the marginal cost to firms. Resources are reallocated to meet the changed consumer preferences. The reverse process when demand falls will release resources from uses which consumers now value less. The opportunity cost of keeping resources in a less popular product becomes too great.

This analysis explains why free market economists want to give maximum possible scope to market forces. They see government intervention and regulation as a dangerous threat to market efficiency. In contrast, interventionist economists see many reasons why the theoretical model doesn't actually correspond to some real-world situations. Intervention can address these issues (see Chapter 7).

Allocative efficiency

Figure 3: The logic of allocative efficiency

Examples

Firms with monopoly power tend to reduce output below ideal levels so use fewer resources but charge higher prices. Externalities and irrational choices (e.g. tobacco) are ignored. Free markets will be inequitable if very uneven income distribution gives a rich minority most income, so resources are used for their wishes whilst others live in poverty.

Productivity

The profit motive and competitive forces both push businesses towards productive efficiency. As profit is total revenue minus total costs, minimising costs will contribute to profitability. In a very price competitive environment, any firm with higher costs than rivals will struggle to survive. The firm minimises its costs by using the fewest resources possible for the quantity produced. This also means that resources for other uses are maximised, so total output can be as high as possible given the resources available. Improving labour productivity is one way of allowing the economy to grow and living standards to rise. When productivity goes up less in the UK than elsewhere, this both restricts growth and makes UK products less competitive.

Competitive-ness

Businesses which are sheltered from competition might have X-inefficiency, making them less productively efficient. For example, managers might be paid according to the total number of people working for them, so they have a perverse incentive to 'waste' labour by employing more workers than are essential. Satisficing might mean a relaxed approach to efficiency if revenue is adequate. Regulated industries might be limited to a profit margin which is a percentage of the capital they employ, giving them an incentive to use more capital than is really necessary. Economies will not inevitably be productively efficient.

The significance of the margin

Many millions of economic decisions are made each day, from the relatively minor such as which filling to have in a sandwich to major decisions on the futures of steel works and nuclear power plants. Alternatives are often similar, with the value of a choice made just being judged as a small margin above the opportunity cost – the best alternative not chosen. As long as the marginal benefit is more than the marginal cost, even slightly more, it is worth making that choice. When we aggregate the choices made by many people, the resource allocation implications become clearer.

Marginal cost and marginal benefit

Example

Newspapers were read in many households in the last century, collected or delivered by newsagents. The leading 10 daily UK newspapers still sold over 12m copies daily in 2001. By May, 2015, that total had fallen below 6.9m. (Source: *The Guardian.*) Some (mainly older) people still take a regular daily paper and many of us will buy and read one occasionally. We might also pick up and read a free paper when one is conveniently available. The habit of reading newspapers is in decline. More people perceive the cost as greater than the benefit (perhaps marginally so). They have changed their habits to rely on alternatives (such as TV and online) or to do without the news.

Opportunity cost

This decline has hit newspaper revenues. With many fixed costs, some struggle to survive. The Independent stopped printing and moved to a digital-only format in March 2016. Advertisers see newspapers getting their message to fewer people, so might expect cheaper rates or might switch to an alternative medium for their message. Fewer trees are pulped for the daily papers. Fewer young people start their day with a delivery round. Some newsagents have stayed viable by building sales of lottery tickets or other items, others have closed. Consequences have rippled out from a marginal change in tastes by millions of people. Individuals have finite spending power and if the opportunity cost of one product seems too high, they will spend their limited funds on something else.

> **Example**
> Marks & Spencer's CEO Steve Rowe understands the margin. In explaining poor clothing sales in the trading period to June, 2016, he told BBC news that the satisfaction customers had been getting had just not matched the clothing prices. He planned better styles and fit, together with lower prices, to offer better value and rebuild market share.

Changing tastes

Changes in tastes and in available information have an impact on what we eat. Consumption of beef in the UK averaged 200 grams per person per week in 1970; this had fallen by almost half by 2015. (Source: DEFRA.) Concerns over excessive red meat consumption have led many people to rely more on chicken, fish or meat-free meals. This has an impact on food purchases and choices from menus. It has been good news for poultry farmers. Globally, the decline in red meat sales in developed countries has been countered by a growing taste for meat as incomes rise in emerging economies. Farmers must respond to the signals they get from market prices if they are to thrive.

> **Think!**
> Identify other consumer trends which have fed through to (a) falling demand, prices and production and (b) rising demand, prices and production.
> How permanent are these trends likely to be?

Trade-offs

When governments set a limit on their expenditure, trade-offs and opportunity costs are inevitable. When austerity is thought necessary, choices seem even harder. Weighing the value of spending on health against social security, education and missile systems, for example, is very complex. There are also short versus long term considerations. In making spending choices, governments must balance what they think right against what they think the electorate will support, whilst interested parties and pressure groups lobby for outcomes to suit their particular preferences. This can be seen as an indirect form of consumer sovereignty. The implications for allocative efficiency can become very complex.

Increasing productivity and productive efficiency

New technologies and capital investment have played a major role in improving labour productivity. Early cars had their body panels knocked into the desired shape by hand-held hammers, in a time consuming process. Now giant body presses require relatively little human effort. BMW uses a body press which produces 17 parts per minute and works for 138 hours per week. The other 30 hours are taken up by resetting for different parts or by maintenance. Two men can control the robots which feed in metal sheets and remove finished parts. Labour productivity has leapt forward as the work has been automated.

Process innovation

Technological innovation sometimes creates new products, 3-D printers, for example. Process innovation, which changes the way we produce existing products, will often improve labour productivity. Computerised technologies have revolutionised many processes. Aircraft are essentially capable of flying without pilots now, though passengers are not thought ready for pilotless transport. Some food outlets now encourage ordering on tablet screens with automatic delivery to a collection point. Less labour intensive processes lift the productivity of remaining workers. Good management delivers more consistent quality.

As countries grow richer they build up their capital stock and the price of capital relative to labour falls. In countries where labour is still relatively cheap, automation has less cost advantage. Sticking with labour intensive methods makes economic sense until the relative costs of labour rise. In a parallel way, poorer households have to prioritise basic needs so have fewer labour saving devices such as dishwashers and coffee machines.

Think!
Identify three products which can be produced in more labour intensive ways in poorer countries. Why might handmade products become fashionable in countries with mass-produced alternatives?

Human capital

Machines are not the only thing getting smarter. Investing in human capital can raise labour productivity. Education, training, skills and experience can all contribute to increased productivity. This applies to managers as well as to workers: they may introduce lean production and teamwork or other productivity-raising developments.

Example
One study (Hendel and Speigel) looked at productivity over a 12-year period in a steel mini-mill producing billets – a simple, homogenous product. There was little turnover in the labour force or new investment, and the mill worked every hour of the year. With little change in conditions, output doubled over the 12 years. Productivity increased for reasons which were hard to identify.

Quality of management

Managers are responsible for the performance of employees in their department. Approaches to managing people, and their effectiveness, will be influenced by the context and there is scope for improvement. (Just think how teachers you have known have varied.) Over time, there has been a general trend for managers to learn, to prepare and to approach their role more systematically; the quality of management has risen.

It would be a mistake to imagine that productivity and productive efficiency always rise. Figure 1 at the start of this chapter shows that UK productivity growth has been well below the long term trend in the last 8 years. Various factors could have contributed to this. Investment in new capital equipment slowed after the financial crisis and recession. When demand is low and fewer sales are possible, many firms have under-utilised capacity. The growth in part-time and temporary work has created some jobs with lower productivity.

Market orientation

The emphasis on non-price competition in many consumer markets spurs regular refinement and innovation. Firms must either accept consumer sovereignty by offering what customers value, or attempt to use the strength of their brand and marketing to persuade people to buy an innovative item. Sometimes even strong and established firms fail to match consumer preferences.

Example
Most bottled water comes from natural springs which are believed to be fresher, purer and healthier than tap water. Many people believe it tastes better too. Major bottled water brands sold in Britain, such as Evian and Buxton, follow this approach. When Coca-Cola introduced Dasani water in 2004, UK consumers found that it was not from a spring but from a tap in Sidcup (London). The tap water was purified and had added trace minerals, but these artificial processes didn't appeal. Problems increased when a cancer-causing agent was identified in the water. Dasani was quickly withdrawn from the UK market.

A firm may spend extensively on developing and launching a new product; the reward can be an impressive profit. The more consumers value a product, the more profitable it is likely to be. This will attract more resources. However, a poor customer response is likely to stop more scarce resources being used in production. Firms can keep themselves market orientated by ensuring that they have done appropriate

Market research

market research before going ahead with a new project. They can focus on delivering 'value' and non-price competition; this frequently involves finding ways to deliver more perceived value.

One of the consequences of this is a gradual improvement in the specifications and performance of many products. We have come to expect, for example, that the fuel consumption of cars, the quality of television pictures and the performance of phone handsets will improve over time. The combination of process innovation, competition and globalisation has delivered a long term fall in the real prices of many electrical goods, clothing items and other products.

The market system can deliver impressive allocative efficiency. Consumers can get the products they want with improving specifications and at attractive prices. Many new product launches fail in the competitive environment, but resources are seldom wasted for long; firms will cut their losses rather than persist with unprofitable ventures.

How markets interact

Intermediate goods

Households are most aware of final goods markets in which products are aimed at consumers. Earlier in supply chains there are **intermediate goods** markets for materials and components traded between firms. Toyota estimated that 30,000 components go into a typical car, counting everything down to individual screws. Seats, for example, are normally bought from a specialist firm rather than made by Toyota. The seat supplier will buy in fabrics, metal and plastic parts from its own suppliers.

Competition in intermediate markets focuses most on price and specification. A supplier which manages to reduce the cost and so the price of a component will be in a very strong position, at least until rivals catch up. Innovation to improve the performance and reliability of a part will be very attractive in intermediate markets. Such developments will feed through into cheaper or better final products. This will work to benefit everyone along the supply chain. It might, for example, lead to an increase in demand for the final product and all the components as well. Market forces are just as active in intermediate markets as in final goods markets, though there tends to be less impulse buying and more rational decision making. Intermediate goods markets are often likely to be allocatively and productively efficient, thanks to competitive pressures.

Supply chains

Besides being heavily interdependent with other members of the same supply chain, firms are also influenced by what goes on in markets for potential substitutes and complements. What goes on in one area or market can have effects which ripple through the economy, perhaps even producing dramatic changes in some places. A business with a brand new technology may cause rival firms to fight for survival.

A new lender

Peer to peer lender Funding Circle was started in 2010 and has averaged more than 100% annual growth. In 2016 it expects to lend more than £1bn. It has become the third biggest lender to UK businesses after RBS and Lloyds Bank. For savers, the return from peer to peer lending is significantly better than most alternatives. For businesses in many sectors there is a new source of funding, making borrowing more accessible. This has made a contribution to start-ups across the economy, adding to competition in many markets. For the high street banks, Funding Circle is a new source of competition, reducing their dominance and forcing them to re-examine their practises.

Exam style question (Section D)

Takeaways

Euromonitor has estimated that in this decade takeaway food sales in the UK will rise by 28% to around £8bn a year. Domino's CEO Dave Wild's simple explanation is that: *"It's the way people live their life today. It's convenient."* This trend has interconnections with many other markets:

● Fewer households have a stay at home 'homemaker' with record numbers in employment.

● Smartphones and tablets are complementary goods used to place orders.

● Another complementary good is entertainment downloads to watch at home.

● Sales of raw ingredients for preparing meals have fallen.

● Supermarkets offer chilled/prepared meals as a substitute for takeaways.

● Meals eaten out are a substitute threatened by this trend.

● Restaurant chains such as Nando's and Burger King now offer home delivery.

● High fat, sugar and calorie takeaways are contributing to obesity problems.

Evaluate links between the growth of takeaway food sales and economic efficiency.   *(20 marks)*

Chapter 6
Market failure

Terms to revise: competitive advantage, market power, price elasticity of demand, barriers to entry,

Collusion

The European Truck Market

The growth of international trade and interdependence has created rapid growth in transportation of materials and products. Within Europe, air, sea and rail each take a small share of business. Trucks (lorries) handle the majority of transport business. Six European producers share 95% of the truck market; they are Daimler, Volvo/Renault, DAF, MAN, Scania and Iveco.

The ACEA (European Automobile Manufacturers Association) has separate directors for truck producers. They have been involved in agreeing new dimension and weight limits for trucks. The first priorities identified in the mission statement are to:

● define and advocate the common interests, policies and positions of the industry, and

● engage in dialogue with the European institutions and other stakeholders in order to advance understanding of industry-related issues, and contribute to effective policy and legislation.

Environmental groups, such as Campaign for Better Transport, have suggested that truck makers are slow to improve fuel consumption and to reduce CO_2 emissions, perhaps colluding to limit innovation to reduce the environmental impact of vehicles. Truck emissions rose by around 36% between 1990 and 2010. There are also allegations that truck producers have colluded on price. MAN, as a whistle-blower, has provided information to EU competition authorities.

Discussion points

How might truck makers benefit from not prioritising better fuel consumption and lower emissions?

What circumstances could support collusion between truck makers?

Explain costs that the alleged collusion could have imposed on others.

Significance of market power

Where consumers have no alternative to buying from a monopoly, the supplier can choose either the price to charge or the quantity to sell. The profit maximising monopolist will set sales at the level where marginal cost is equal to marginal revenue (see page 20). This can involve **abnormal profits**, especially if demand is price inelastic. The quantity sold will be kept lower than in a competitive market so the product will be scarcer than ideal and more expensive. This is market failure: market forces fail to deliver efficient outcomes.

Abnormal profit

> **Abnormal profit** is profit in excess of normal profit, i.e. that needed to keep the firm in business. Abnormal profit is generally the result of market power. In near-perfect markets only normal profit can be earned.

Differentiation and branding by an oligopolist have a major objective of increasing market share for the business. This can involve innovation to improve products and processes in ways which bring better and possibly cheaper products to consumers. So this is a powerful form of competition that can enhance allocative and productive efficiency. However, there can also be other consequences.

Reducing PED

If a firm succeeds in building a distinctive image, brand loyalty and a significant market share, this will reduce price elasticity of demand and create market power. This could enable a firm to charge higher prices and perhaps to use anti-competitive means to further strengthen its position.

Think!

Do you have brand loyalty for some products? If so, why?

Does your loyalty mean you pay more than prices of other brands?

Brand development vs. consumer sovereignty

Very strong brands are trusted by their loyal customers to the extent that Steve Jobs (of Apple) could say *"A lot of times, people don't know what they want until you show it to them."* This turns the idea of consumer sovereignty on its head. If trusted brands can lead consumer thinking, then suppliers have power over resource allocation. Where top brands thrive with an exclusive and expensive image, low prices might be damaging and cost minimisation not a priority.

> **Example**
> One school in Switzerland claimed the USP that it was the world's most expensive. If any other school increased fees to a similar level, the school simply raised its own prices by more. Some parents trusted that as the most expensive it must be the best. Cost cutting was not considered.

If firms abuse market power, they are able to distort resource allocation whilst increasing their own profits at the expense of consumers. By taking more of consumer' incomes, they reduce real consumer spending power and so people's standard of living. This is an example of market failure, of markets not generating efficient outcomes. This chapter covers the ways in which market power may be abused.

Restrictive practices

Where a dominant firm has monopoly power, or where firms collude, they can take advantage of market power by acting to reduce competition. **Collusion** means making a private agreement to act in a way that restricts output or raises prices or both. **Restrictive practices** include:

● Restricting supply and increasing prices.

● Market sharing – colluding businesses divide up the market, sometimes geographically, so that there is less competition in all areas.

Price fixing

● Price fixing, where suppliers agree to sell at the same price, so that they do not compete.

All of these are anti-competitive practices. Once a situation has been created in which consumers have little real choice, higher prices will deter relatively few buyers as PED is likely to be relatively low, so revenue and profits should increase.

> **Collusion** means collaborating to take joint action. In markets, collusion generally reduces competition.
>
> Any anti-competitive abuse of market power is a **restrictive practice**. Examples include artificial barriers to entry, fixing prices, deciding how to share markets (market rigging) and bundling. products together.

Many restrictive practices involve collusion between supposedly rival firms which act together in order to create and exploit market power. OPEC (The Organisation of Petroleum Exporting Countries) members agreed for decades to limit their supply in order to push up prices. The growth of output from non-members (e.g. US fracking) has reduced OPEC's power.

If firms can find a way to erect or reinforce **barriers to entry**, it gets harder for new entrants to challenge their dominance. A barrier, for example, could be control of a vital input for production or tying retailers to selling only approved brands. For decades, the De Beers Group bought up as much of global diamond production as possible, allowing them to dominate and control the market.

Tying together or '**bundling**' products also reduces competition. The predominance of its operating systems allowed Microsoft to bundle its own web browser with operating systems. This made it difficult for rival browsers to compete. Abuse of patent law or a reputation for aggressive legal action can also block or deter competitors.

Restrictive practices can involve agreements on where to trade or who to trade with. Sometimes, firms have agreed to 'carve up' geographical areas and not compete in rivals' territories. Producers have tied retailers to exclusive contracts, cutting out rival suppliers. Resale price maintenance deals fix retail prices. A retailer which refuses to co-operate can be cut out by suppliers' refusing to trade with them. There are many ways in which collusion can make life less competitive, more comfortable and more profitable for firms. Consumers are left with higher prices and/or less choice.

Bid rigging

> **Example**
>
> Twenty years ago, US authorities auctioned radio spectrum licenses for mobile phone operators in 493 cities and areas. Companies found a way to signal each other and rig the bidding. Each area had a code. When a rival made a bid for an area (say 256) which one of the businesses involved wanted, the firm responded by making a bid for an area the rival was thought to want, with a price ending in the digits 256. The message was: 'we want 256, if you bid on it we'll bid for places you want'.

> **Find out**
>
> Identify a business that appears to have market power and is keeping prices higher than they need be. Explain how it is possible to do this. Explain how this may be distorting the allocation of resources.

Cartels and collusion

Adam Smith

The first recognised economist, Adam Smith, noted in the late 18th Century that *"people of the same trade seldom meet together... without the conversation ending in a conspiracy against the public, or in some contrivance to raise prices"* (Wealth of Nations, 1776).

Smith was writing when most markets were localised; many consumers had no alternative to buying from local traders and craftsmen. Most towns were smaller, there might only have been a few bakers or carpenters in a community. If such suppliers colluded, this created a shared monopoly. They gained by agreeing on prices and other aspects of business, rather than competing.

Cartels may agree high prices and share higher profits than a competitive environment would allow.

Improvements in transportation, marketing and recently e-commerce have given consumers access to a wide range of suppliers. This can prevent collusion if there are simply too many suppliers to co-ordinate effectively. Some industries are intensely competitive, with fierce rivalry and extensive choice for consumers. In other cases, markets are dominated by national or global oligopolies. This means a limited number of suppliers with large market shares. As with the tradespeople in Smith's time, there is again the potential for collusion – such as the truck makers' deal (page 29).

The largest individual firms have market power in many oligopolies, but their ability to exploit this is limited if similar rivals compete vigorously. A bigger danger in oligopoly is of large firms forming a **cartel** to exploit shared monopoly power. Competition law makes this illegal in many countries. Collusion is therefore likely to be covert, kept secret to avoid punishment. We cannot know exactly how many cartels there are, but we do know that prosecutions bring cases to light fairly regularly.

> A **cartel** is a formal, secret, agreement between a number of producers of a good or service, usually involving restrictive practices such as manipulation of prices. As cartels are normally illegal, they are more likely to be **covert** (secret) rather than **overt** (open).
>
> Where there is no agreement, there can be **tacit collusion**, with no cartel, if firms each independently work out that anti-competitive behaviour is in their interests.

Cartels may agree high prices and share higher profits than a competitive environment would allow. Cartel members might suppress innovations which threaten their comfortable existence. Or they might rig bids for contracts, taking turns to submit high bids whilst alternative bids come from the other firms, which set them even higher. Even without a cartel, tacit collusion can result in firms' behaving anti-competitively so markets fail to operate efficiently.

> **Example**
> In 2009, the OFT (Office of Fair Trading) claimed that 112 building companies had engaged in bid rigging. This involved building projects across England including schools, universities, hospitals, and numerous private projects. Nine companies were not punished as evidence against them was insufficient. One hundred and three construction firms were fined as a result.

Figure 1: The things cartels do

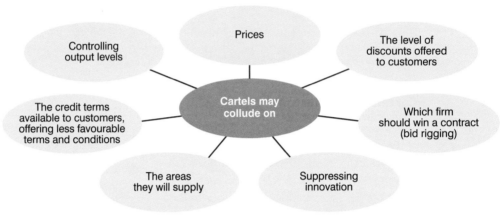

Types of collusion

Monopsony

Every transaction has a buyer and a seller. The focus in market failure is often on supply, but buyers can also have market power. This is monopsony power. The example of monopsony which has attracted most attention in the UK is of supermarkets buying from small farmers. A large supermarket will often buy the entire crop of a farm. The farm shapes its processes and output, and perhaps focuses on a single product, to suit the buyer. Once this position is reached, the buyer has a very powerful position on future contract negotiations.

> **Monopsony power** exists where a major purchaser has market power over smaller suppliers which can be dominated by the buyer.

Dealing with suppliers

Monopsony buyers can exert power in other ways. In 2016, for example, the grocery code adjudicator (watchdog) ordered Tesco to make 'significant changes' in dealings with suppliers. Suppliers had waited up to two years for payment, which were sometimes cut for unexpected reasons. (Source: *The Guardian*, 26 January 2016.) Once again, there is likely to be an impact on efficiency in markets if power is abused.

> **Example**
> Kiwi fruit are produced by many growers in New Zealand but 'Zespri' handles storage and sales, with a monopsony on buying from growers. Kiwifruit New Zealand (KNZ) regulate that monopsony:
> *"Our role… is to safeguard the interests of growers by ensuring Zespri works in their best interests and to ensure it meets its international trading obligations."*

Natural monopolies

Competition would be wasteful with natural monopolies, so the sole supplier has market power. Many natural monopolies are related to infrastructure. To have multiple competing networks of gas and water pipes or railway tracks would waste scarce resources. Such industries were once in the public sector in most countries and still are in some.

China has its State-owned Assets Supervision and Administration Commission (SASAC), a body responsible for managing 117 large SOEs (State Owned Enterprises). Many Western countries have had privatisation programmes since the 1980s. The water, gas, electricity and rail networks were included in UK privatisations, for example. One objective was to improve efficiency by increasing the role of market forces in such industries.

Natural monopolies

Private sector natural monopolies, such as UK water companies, will seek to minimise costs if they are profit maximisers. This should bring productive efficiency. However, with no market pressures to ensure competitive pricing, allocative efficiency is not guaranteed. Water prices were the fastest growing component of the retail price index for three decades after privatisation. The firms were required to invest in improving their networks but they were also very profitable.

Natural monopolies also exist where limited demand and economies of scale give a single supplier a cost advantage. A single supplier can be more productively efficient. How much the firm can exploit their monopoly power will depend on PED for the product. There are single producers of effective treatments for rare health problems. PED is low and prices potentially very high. Glybera is a gene therapy that treats people with a one in a million problem. In 2015 it was priced at €1.1m per course of treatment.

The labour market

Monopoly and monopsony power can be found in labour markets. The public sector employs a significant proportion of workers in many countries, often 30-50% of the labour force. Employers' associations may create shared monopsony power. In many towns there is a large business with a major share of local employment and so monopsony power. Professional associations and trade unions sometimes have monopoly power.

Monopoly and monopsony power

> **Example**
> The dispute over junior hospital doctor contracts in 2015-16 illustrates labour market power. The NHS (ultimately the government) employs most doctors so has monopsony power. 38,000 of the 55,000 UK junior doctors belong to the British Medical Association (BMA), so it has monopoly power. Weekend working and total hours were discussed most, but overall earnings (and costs) were important in the dispute. Contract changes were proposed in 2012. Both sides felt they had the power to prevail. Demand for NHS doctors depends on political decisions; supply is dominated by the BMA. Free market theory has little relevance here.

Parts of the labour market have very one sided power. Extreme cases include 'modern slavery', where people are coerced into long hours, little pay and poor living standards. Victims may have limited education or confidence, been trafficked into the country and told to 'work off a debt'. This can be domestic slavery. 'Gangmasters' who organise agricultural workers have bullied people. Trafficked immigrants may be forced to become sex workers.

At the opposite extreme, it may be difficult to recruit anyone. If there is only one real choice, the supplier can sometimes set their own price. Professional associations or unions can have monopoly power; regulations might control access to types of work. Unqualified dentists cannot set up in business; this gives qualified dentists market power.

Reducing monopoly or monopsony power can lead to a better balance. However, if the limited power of the weaker side is reduced this can make markets less efficient or fair. French labour law has sometimes been thought to weaken the relative position of employers. Where trade unions are banned or have very limited power, employees will be in a relatively weak position.

Government actions also have an impact on the working of labour markets. A national minimum (or living) wage sets a floor below which hourly rates cannot go. This could cause greater reliance on young workers or apprentices, who are cheaper to employ. There have been suggestions that heavy tax rates can distort markets for the highest paid workers, pushing pay up or encouraging evasion to offset the impact of tax.

Implications of market failure

Where markets work effectively, the invisible hand of market forces needs no government intervention. If competitive pressure forces firms to minimise costs, there should be productive efficiency. If the benefit of the last unit made balances its cost, there will be allocative efficiency.

Imperfect markets

Imperfect markets often do not achieve allocative or productive efficiency. Market power allows vested interests to reach selfish decisions, creating private gains from abnormal profits, at the expense of consumers or competing firms. Any action that increases prices is also likely to cut sales, so consumers pay higher prices and consume less.

New technologies, in computing and elsewhere, have brought many new, cheaper and better products. This benefits consumers and society. At the same time, patent holding, economies of scale and non-price competition have created some global businesses with extensive market power.

Examples include Amazon, Apple, Facebook, Google and Microsoft. Each has effective differentiation and large market shares in their successful areas. Apple and Google (Alphabet) have been the two most profitable businesses in the world recently. In 2015 Apple's accounts showed turnover of $233.7bn and profit of $53.4bn. These totals and the profit margin of almost 23% indicate how powerful this business is.

Many Apple product consumers are happy with their purchases and firmly loyal. In a market with many small competing firms, it would have been difficult for any one firm to resource such rapid innovation in smartphones or to match the design strengths of current models. However, if competition had forced Apple to operate at lower prices, allocative efficiency might have improved. Lower prices might have increased pressure for productive efficiency.

Government power

Governments have market power, e.g. as monopsonies in the labour market or in defence procurement. This power could be used to drive wages or prices below efficient levels. Government has monopoly power over services supplied by the public sector. If public sector provision is inadequate or goes beyond supplying efficient quantities, this is a market failure.

Exam style question (Paper 3)

Indian cement

In 2012, the Indian competition authority (CCI) investigated complaints that cement oligopolists had colluded to fix prices. The leading cement producers were fined the equivalent of more than £650m. Cement companies have used legal proceedings to contest both the judgement and the fines and the case is protracted. A new hearing into the original complaint was ordered late in 2015.

Again in 2015, a builders' trade body made fresh allegations of a cartel between cement producers. They said that cement prices had risen by 20-40% in 2 months, despite falling costs and low demand.

Source: Adapted from *The Financial Express*

Questions

a) Discuss plausible causes of an oligopoly in Indian cement supply. *(8 marks)*

b) Assess the evidence used to support allegations of a fresh cartel. *(10 marks)*

c) Assess the possible impact of the alleged cartel on allocative efficiency. *(12 marks)*

d) Evaluate the extent to which productive efficiency is likely to be lost if there is a cartel which raises prices in such an industry. *(20 marks)*

Chapter 7

Business regulation

Modelling collusion

In May, 2016, The Competition and Markets Authority (CMA) accused five leading UK model agencies of price fixing and overcharging over a two year period from April 2013 to March 2015. FM Models, Models 1, Premier, Storm and Viva are alleged to have operated a secret cartel and exchanged confidential, competitively sensitive information, including future pricing information, sometimes agreeing a common approach to pricing. The Association of Model Agents (AMA), representing the firms involved, is accused of a key role in this conspiracy. The CMA alleges that the AMA systematically circulated email alerts to members encouraging the agencies to reject fees being offered by specific customers and to negotiate more. The CMA's Stephen Blake said: "The allegations concern prices charged to a range of customers, including high street chains, online fashion retailers and consumer goods brands. The CMA alleges that these five model agencies sought to achieve higher prices in negotiations with their customers by colluding instead of competing."

Source: CMA

Discussion points

How could these model agencies have gained by operating a cartel?

How could the CMA prove that there had been collusion?

How should collusion, such as is alleged here, be punished?

Promoting competition: preventing restrictive practices

Restrictive practices disadvantage consumers and can reduce both productive and allocative efficiency. Authorities take action against restrictive practices. In the UK, this was the responsibility of the OFT (Office of Fair Trading) until 2014. The CMA (Competition and Markets Authority) took over from both the OFT and the Competition Commission (CC). This allowed some streamlining and simplification of the system.

CMA

In the EU, the UK has had additional protection from EU Competition Commissioner Margrethe Vestager's team. Until the UK leaves the EU, the CMA basically has authority within the UK, whereas the EU team focus on EU-wide issues. Where there have been overlaps, collaboration has worked well. Both the CMA and the Commission have enforced controls on restrictive practices, ending and punishing illegal action by cartels or individual firms. They both sought to encourage competition and efficiency, whilst protecting consumers from abuse of market power.

EU Competition Commission

As many markets are globalised, collaboration also takes place with other bodies such as the US Federal Trade Commission. Despite variations in approach, competition authorities share the same basic concerns.

Examples

In April 2011 the OFT fined Reckitt Benckiser £10.2 million after finding it had abused its dominant position in the market for the NHS supply of heartburn medicines. The OFT found that Reckitt Benckiser withdrew and de-listed Gaviscon Original Liquid from NHS use, forcing prescribers to choose a more expensive option.

In 2009, to resolve EU competition concerns, Microsoft agreed to offer users of its operating systems a browser choice, allowing them to download browsers from other suppliers. In March, 2013, The EU fined Microsoft €561 million for failing to offer the promised choice. The total of EU fines issued against Microsoft over the past decade is more than €2.2 billion.

Regulators

One problem for regulators is that whilst overt collusion (see pages 15-16) is clearly illegal, covert cartel activity can be difficult to prove. Trails of electronic messages can offer strong evidence. Often, though, the best evidence is confession. A 'whistle-blower' involved in collusion can give full detail. Whistle-blowers or the first firm to confess are treated leniently, often escaping punishment. This gives firms an incentive to co-operate with the authorities and can even spark a race to confess if cartel members cease to trust each other.

Price fixing

Example
British Airways and Virgin Atlantic agreed to fix the same fuel surcharges after a fuel price rise. Virgin Atlantic subsequently became a whistle-blower over this act of collusion. BA agreed to pay a fine of £121.5 million whilst no punishment was levied on Virgin. Four BA executives went to criminal trial over this in 2010, but the case collapsed.

Tacit collusion, where firms independently work out that non-competitive action is in their interest, is harder to stop. In such cases, the CMA can still initiate action to free up competition despite the absence of cartel activity.

Tacit collusion

Example
In May 2016, UK retail banks were instructed to offer clearer information to customers, making comparisons between banks simpler. There was no evidence of a cartel agreement, but the CMA judged that poor quality of information contributed to consumer reluctance to change banks.

Promoting competition: controlling mergers and takeovers

Mergers and takeovers remove at least one competitor from the market and can create monopoly power. The CMA investigates mergers or takeovers which would create a market share of 25% or more, or a business with turnover of more than £70 million p.a. If a merger is thought to have no adverse impact on competition or the public interest, it is allowed. Where there is potential damage to competition the CMA can impose conditions to reduce damage or can block a merger or takeover.

Example
In 2015 Poundland (with 600 shops) launched a takeover of 99p Stores (250 shops). The CMA expressed concerns that the deal could reduce competition in more than 90 places. After a six month inquiry process, the CMA accepted that the combined company would still face competition from many directions so consumers *"would not face a reduction in choice, value or quality of service."* The takeover was allowed to proceed.

EU action

EU competition authorities have had responsibility if a 'community-wide' impact was identified or when two firms involved had turnover above €250 million. Activities were well harmonised, with national and EU bodies working together. Consequences of unpicking this are considered later, pages 43-4.

Example
In 2016 Hong Kong based Hutchinson, owner of '3', agreed to buy the UK O2 phone operation from Telefonica, for £10.3 billion. Both phone regulator Ofcom and the CMA expressed concerns about this merger and a reduction from four to three network operators. The European Commission blocked the sale; Margrethe Vestager said *"We want the mobile telecoms sector to be competitive, so that consumers can enjoy innovative mobile services at fair prices and high network quality."*

Promoting competition: privatisation

Public sector organisations are often protected from effective competition and are less efficient. NHS hospitals and the police, for example, don't sell their services for profit in a conventional way. With no charge for many services, they are largely funded from government income. Some professional observers say that without market pressure to control costs, they could become wasteful and inefficient.

Many public sector workers deliver the very best performance they can, but some problems have been identified. Productive efficiency is lost if costs are not minimised and allocative efficiency is not guaranteed

Some analysts suggested that Royal Mail was sold too cheaply.

when political decisions govern choices over priorities. Those wanting minimal government tend to favour privatisation. Others prefer more public sector involvement, distrust privatisation and feel that public assets were sold off too cheaply.

Towering inefficiency or public assets

Think!
"At the time it was privatised BT had 250,000 customers waiting for a telephone line to be installed. The public telephone boxes doubled as public lavatories. Electricity and gas prices went down before elections, and up after them. In the water industry, the sewers were crumbling, the beaches a disgrace, the rivers were filthy, and water shortages commonplace. The public images of British Rail, its timetables regularly undone by 'the wrong sort of snow' and leaves on the line, was of grubby trains and surly staff."

Extracted from: 'The National Wealth – Who Gets What in Britain'

The Government has historically undervalued State owned assets when privatising them and this trend is continuing...The lack of transparency and integrity in privatisation deals should be causing all UK citizens to question the logic and benefits of privatisation. If the Government were a publicly traded company, the Board of Directors would likely face prosecution for failure of their fiduciary responsibility to the shareholders (i.e. the UK taxpayers).

Extracted from aviewfromtheattic.com

Some analysts suggested that Royal Mail was sold too cheaply. Find out how Royal Mail performed before and after privatisation.

Privatisations began in the early 1980s with Jaguar and BT, followed by British Aerospace, gas, steel, water, electricity, coal and railways. Activities staying largely in the public sector, such as defence, health and education have had non-core services such as catering and cleaning outsourced.

The BT experience

The effect of privatisation on efficiency has varied between industries. This is hard to measure and there are wide differences of opinion on the overall success. After privatisation BT shed around 150,000 workers with little decline in service standards, suggesting that productive efficiency improved. Innovation also increased. However, BT has also faced criticism; the train operators even more so. Privatisation went into reverse in the financial crisis when some banks were nationalised to avoid bankruptcy. They will return to the private sector. Smaller organisations such as the Land Registry are currently in the privatisation pipeline.

BT, gas, water and electricity all have distribution networks which are natural monopolies. Gas, electricity, phone services and railways have a system of competing retail businesses sharing infrastructure maintained by a single firm. These infrastructure monopolies have no direct competition so regulation is necessary to prevent abuse of their market power.

Regulating natural monopolies

The main UK regulators for natural monopolies are OFCOM (communications), OFGEM (gas and electricity), ORR (rail and road) and OFWAT (water). Regulators have a difficult task. They target prices and standards, allowing suppliers to make a healthy but not excessive profit, whilst protecting consumers from exploitation and encouraging efficiency. So, for example, they often require prices to rise by less than the rate of inflation. This pushes firms to improve productive efficiency and cut costs so as to maintain or increase profits.

Water issues

Ageing water infrastructure had leaks and faults so water suppliers were allowed price increases above inflation to fund investment. One estimate has water bills rising by 50% more than inflation since privatisation (Source: corporatewatch.org.) Investment has also risen, but infrastructure

Ageing water infrastructure had leaks and faults so water suppliers were allowed price increases above inflation to fund investment.

problems persist. OFWAT now has a tougher pricing regime and improved performance targets.

> **Example**
> In 2016 water regulator OFWAT wants water companies to reduce real prices by 5% by 2020 and to improve their leak fixing performance. The price cutting is aimed at combining productive efficiency with savings for customers. Rising water prices previously brought increased profits to the firms involved whilst taking a growing chunk of household incomes.

Regulatory capture

There have been accusations of 'regulatory capture' – regulators being bombarded with one-sided information from their industry and persuaded to treat firms generously at the expense of customers. In the absence of market forces, regulator judgement plays a major role in determining levels of efficiency and pricing.

Protecting consumers

Many purchases are made with little information. Some consumers make a detailed study of potential purchases and most are bombarded with marketing information (that may be correct). However, we lack full knowledge to protect ourselves from firms that might make misleading or exaggerated claims, cut corners or create hazards.

Consumer choices

Some consumers take obvious risks. Gamblers overestimate their chances of winning, so impoverishing themselves. Smokers smoke despite evidence of harm. People buy foodstuffs that contribute to obesity. It is difficult to regulate adult purchases of harmful goods and services.

> **Example**
> Supply chains for many products, including foods, have grown longer and more complex. In 2013 it emerged that horsemeat was being sold as beef in UK supermarkets. This shocked UK consumers. The supermarkets quickly withdrew products and promised better controls. The Food Safety Authority in Ireland first identified the problem. UK authorities have since taken more interest in meat products.

Fake goods

When firms work hard to build a positive and expensive image for their brands, it is no surprise that others try to cash in on this. A Rolex watch sold for £10, or a Chanel perfume for £5, is probably counterfeit. Some counterfeiting has serious implications for safety. If car brake components or a cycling helmet are sub-standard, buyers put themselves and others at risk. Fake drugs or cosmetics can seriously damage users. Global online marketing bypasses conventional supply chains and so brings increased dangers.

Consumer protection

Consumer protection law states that products must be as described and fit for their intended purpose. Public health is protected through regulations relating to food. Action can be taken against businesses that:

● mislead consumers into buying products or services.

● sell unsafe or dangerous items.

● don't carry out work properly, e.g. leaving a home in a dangerous state.

● sell fake or counterfeit items.

● pressure people into buying something they don't want to buy.

Limited funding

2016 budgets for trading standards in England and Wales are 40% lower than they were in 2010. Regulators now have to choose targets for their limited resources. The CMA is responsible for ensuring that contract terms are fair and pricing strategies do not mislead.

It would be unrealistic for buyers to expect legal protection in all circumstances. The ancient principle of 'caveat emptor' (let the buyer beware) still has value. Risky or foolish purchases can bring expense or danger. There is little or no protection for purchases from private individuals rather than traders, and problems with vendors in remote and distant lands are seldom resolved.

Employee protection

Employees might have little choice about who they work for or the conditions of work where employers have market power. Cost cutting could mean short-cuts on health and safety, conditions of work or job security. There is a trade-off between the interests of employers and employees. With redundancies for example, some employers value the ability to reduce worker numbers quickly and cheaply, but risk and uncertainty for workers is reduced by redundancy procedures and payments.

Health and safety

There is not just a simple trade-off here. Many employers believe that giving employees security and good working conditions will generate benefits from better motivation and performance which more than cover the costs involved. Some employers are ready to treat employees well, but resent the bureaucracy and red tape involved in checking working conditions or health and safety compliance.

Trade-offs

> **Example**
> In March 2016, supermarket chain Aldi and contractors Wilkinson Maintenance were fined after a smoking shelter injured a worker. A gust of wind moved an unsecured smoking shelter, briefly pinning him. He had soft-tissue injuries to his back and both arms, and then nightmares about the incident. Aldi was fined £100,000 and Wilkinson Maintenance £20,000.
> Source: Shoponline.co.uk

The legal basis for UK employee protection has evolved through many Acts of Parliament. The Health and Safety Executive takes a lead in its specialist area. Employees are entitled to at least the set minimum (living) wage, to protection from unfair dismissal, to work in a safe environment, to join a union if they wish, to take maternity or paternity leave and to have holidays.

In the trade-off between labour market flexibility and employee protection, the UK was sometimes pushed by the EU to protect employees more than some politicians might have chosen. Working long hours was associated with ill-health and stress. So, for example, part of the EU 'Social Chapter' is a directive setting a maximum 48 hour working week (with some opt-outs). The UK government first contested its obligation to enforce this, but it came into force in the UK in 1998. After leaving the EU, UK governments will be able to make changes which unpick obligations under EU directives.

Think!

Do you see health and safety at work as part of an essential safety net?

"If your only source of information was the UK's tabloid press you would see health and safety as a nuisance." – Judith Hackitt, chair of Health and Safety Executive.

"We don't want to turn the safety net into a hammock that lulls able-bodied people into complacency and dependence." – Paul Ryan.

Exam style question (Section C)

Improving competition in the energy market

A Competition and Markets Authority (CMA) investigation into the energy market found that UK customers may have paid about £1.7bn a year more than they would have done with effective competition.

Measures taken in 2016 to increase competition and drive down prices included:

- a price cap for households using pre-payment meters. These are often poor households and have paid relatively high prices.

- a database of customers paying standard rates for three years, to be held by regulator Ofgem and open to other suppliers.

- ending the limit to a maximum of four tariffs per supplier.

- strengthening the ability of price comparison sites to help consumers.

- ending the use of 'rollover contracts' which switch customers to dearer tariffs when fixed term deals end.

The 'Which' consumer magazine welcomed help for pre-pay meter customers but feared that the main result of the proposed database could be a rise in unwanted marketing.

Sources: gov.co.uk and 'Which' May 2016

Using the information provided above and earlier in this chapter, evaluate the likely impact of these measures on competition in the energy market. *(20 marks)*

Chapter 8
How much regulation?

Private Healthcare

Since 2012, the CMA and its predecessor, the Competition Commission, have been investigating private healthcare, with particular emphasis on London. A report in April 2014 found that features of the market had an adverse effect on competition. Some recommendations have been implemented. The 'Private Healthcare Information Network' now offers independent information for private patients. There has been a crackdown on benefits and incentive schemes provided to doctors for referring patients to particular hospital operators.

In 2014, the CMA found that there was insufficient competition in London, allowing higher prices to medical insurers than would be expected in a well-functioning market. HCA International Limited, the largest private hospital operator in central London, was required to sell one or two hospitals. HCA appealed against this and the CMA has now reconsidered. It now anticipates possible new entrants to the market to make it more competitive. A final MCA report on this market is expected later this year.

Discussion points

Are businesses happier without regulators investigating their markets?

What is wrong with private hospitals paying doctors for referring patients to them?

How long should a CMA investigation process take?

The benefits of regulation

Market failure

Unregulated markets may fail. Where market power or restrictive practices exist, suppliers can exploit the situation to their own advantage. This is likely to work against both consumer interests and efficiency. To prevent this there is a legal framework that gives guidance on what is acceptable and unacceptable and enforces the law. Enforcement involves preventing illegal activity and punishing wrongdoers. HCA's appeal shows how businesses may react to CMA conclusions: enforcement is rarely easy. But it does set an example.

Powerful businesses would prefer less regulation and more freedom to exploit their strength. Most businesses dislike the costs and bureaucracy involved in regulation. However, firms up and down the supply chain benefit from action against the abuse of power. A clear example of this is in the way that controlling supermarkets' ability to use monopsony power helps small suppliers. The Groceries Code Adjudicator role was introduced in 2013 specifically to focus on the relationship between supermarkets and suppliers. Many firms see ways in which regulation works to their advantage.

Think!

The Alton Towers 'Smiler' ride is 1,170 metres long and reaches 85kmph. In June 2015, two carriages collided and four people were seriously injured. Two of them required leg amputations. An operator had manually overridden the safety system. Owners Merlin Entertainments admitted breaches of health and safety rules in areas such as training. A record fine is expected by the time you read this. Find out how large the fine was in this case.

Does the fine seem appropriate to you?

How can the risk of future accidents best be controlled?

Super-complaints

Designated bodies which work on behalf of consumers can raise 'super-complaints' with the CMA. These are the Consumers' Association (Which), Citizens' Advice, Energywatch, the Consumer Council for Water, CAMRA (real ale), Postwatch and the General Consumer Council for Northern Ireland. This gives consumer representatives a way to draw attention to situations where the structure of a market or the conduct of firms appears to work against the interests of consumers.

Regulation benefits

Example

A Citizens' Advice super-complaint in 2005 against the pricing of Payment Protection Insurance (PPI) and selling of inappropriate policies eventually led to compensation payments in excess of £20bn.

In 2014, 'Which' complained about confusing and misleading special offers in supermarkets. This led to changes. Asda, for example, agreed not to use 'now' prices for longer than 'was' prices, to ensure that multibuy offers are better value than single products, and not to immediately follow multibuys with 'was/now' offers.

There is little doubt that regulation improves consumer protection. Individuals cannot check the safety of every transport operator they use or the precise contents of everything they buy. Where natural monopolies are privatised, regulation is essential to avoid excess exploitation of market power. There is an important function for official bodies responsible for checking the ways in which markets operate and the safety of the community. (The CMA's intervention on private healthcare aims to protect consumers.)

The costs of regulation

Regulation faces three main criticisms. Some people say:

- It is a waste of resources both in the public sector and for businesses. Providing and maintaining a safe working environment, paying the living wage, and meeting required product standards can all add to costs and so push up prices.
- Compliance with regulations can cause delays and entail increased costs.

Government failure

- Regulation is often ineffective and misguided, with government failure often adding to market failure rather than curing it, making situations worse rather than better. A blocked merger, for example, might have led to economies of scale, lower prices and British firms becoming more competitive.

The 'Nanny State' objection adds that people should be free to make their own decisions and mistakes. Seen from this angle, interference with personal and corporate freedoms is seen as generally wrong. FOREST, the pro-smoking organisation, consistently takes this approach. Most regulation is opposed by some people. For example, speed limits cause resentment in some drivers.

Think!

Do you approve of regulations such as wearing crash helmets on motor bikes and seat belts in cars? Which legal restriction do you see as least justified?

Are there local regulations in your school or college which seem petty and unnecessary?

Why do so many rules and regulations exist?

Example

The privatised Royal Mail is required to offer a universal service at a uniform price. In other words, they must deliver letters to any UK address, regardless of distance, at a standard price. Regulators (Postcomm and now Ofcom) have been keen to introduce competition to more profitable parts of the postal service in order to promote efficiency. Both Royal Mail and the CWU (postpersons' union) argue that allowing others to syphon off the most profitable activities without taking any share of the costly parts of universal service reduces the quality of service and is unsustainable.

More or less regulation?

The Institute of Economic Affairs described the UK as *"the third worst country in the EU for nanny state interference"* with *"the number three spot as the most meddling country in the EU."* Excessive regulation and punitive 'sin taxes' were seen as largely to blame. *"Although paternalistic laws are often said to be justified on health grounds, analysis of the figures found no link between nanny state regulation and longer life expectancy."*

Source iea.org.uk, March 2016

The Economist reports that only the USA and Canada are less regulated then the UK.

Competition vs. global market power

Anti-competitive behaviour was easier in Adam Smith's times, since limitations on transport and trade kept competition local. Globalisation and open economies reduce the scope for anti-competitive behaviour within one country as high profits can attract rivals from other countries and continents. The strong link between the growth of trade and economic growth is partly explained by the power of competition to force firms to operate efficiently. As there is less scope for anti-competitive behaviour in an open economy there should also be less need for regulation. However, there are now multinationals with global market power. Lengthy supply chains increase the risks of 'cheating' by distant firms. Nike and Primark have been accused in the past of ignoring poor working conditions in overseas supplier companies.

Government attempts to reduce spending and the public sector deficit since 2010 have brought significant cuts. For example, the CMA was formed in 2014 with around 800 staff, slightly more than the number previously working at the OFT but significantly less than the OFT and Competition Commission combined. This has reduced the capacity for action but has pleased those who believe in 'small government' with minimum public expenditure and taxation.

> **Think!**
>
> The banking sector has always been relatively strongly regulated. Despite the regulation, the banking crisis of 2007/8 created a major recession and left nationalisation as the only practical way to save Royal Bank of Scotland and Lloyds. Part of the problem was that regulators had not kept up with digital age developments in the industry. To prevent another crisis, much more regulation has been put in place.
>
> Why is it important to regulate banking activity? Think of two separate reasons.

Leaving the EU

EU regulation

The CMA's two tier system, investigating mergers and restrictive practices, (pages 35-6), has served consumers well in some ways. The EU action against truck makers, like the Commission's readiness to take on global businesses such as Microsoft, works in the interests of UK consumers. However, there has frequently been criticism of EU regulation.

> **Think!**
>
> **The European Truck Market (part 2, part 1 on page 29)**
> The EU probe into the behaviour of truck companies between 1997 and 2011 found that heavy vehicle fuel efficiency had stagnated since the mid-1990s, there had been collusion on price fixing and agreement on the timing and price increases for introduction of new fuel technologies. "Extremely high" fines are likely and some hauliers are considering damage claims.
>
> Is the EU more capable of regulating this market than national bodies like the CMA?

In the run up to the EU referendum, one sample issue was the cancellation of a hundred year old event, The Stert island Swim, off Burnham-on-Sea in Somerset. EU regulations on bathing water were not met as the water was too polluted. People could still have swum at their own risk, but the event organisers were concerned that insurance cover would be invalidated so cancelled the swim. Some locals saw this as Brussels officialdom infringing their liberties. Others felt a better reaction might be to press for action to reduce the sewage and other pollutants in the water.

An EU ruling that unusually bent bananas should be classed as sub-standard was (wrongly) reported as a ban on bent bananas and ridiculed. This is an area where the need for regulation is less clear-cut, though UK supermarkets believe their customers are less happy with unusually shaped or coloured fruit and vegetables so they impose strict standards on their suppliers.

Climate change

EU targets for combatting climate change, such as achieving a 20% share of energy from renewable sources by 2020, have a reputed cost of £4.7bn a year. The target of a 20% cut in greenhouse gas emissions with a 20% improvement in energy efficiency imposes more constraints. One element in this was imposing new standards for the efficiency of vacuum cleaners. A 'triumph', in some eyes, is that Parliament will be able to restore the right to buy inefficient and power-hungry vacuum cleaners if it chooses to. Those who are concerned about climate change suggest that UK governments have sometimes been slower to make reforms to protect the environment than the EU has. They see a danger of backward steps in the post-EU era.

Find out

Do environmental groups (e.g. Greenpeace) prefer the UK being outside the EU?

Have there been contentious changes in regulation recently?

What effect might the 'Brexit' process have on the regulated businesses?

Labour market flexibility

Another contentious area is the trade-off between employment protection and labour market flexibility. Once the UK has left the EU, Parliament will have the power to repeal rulings in areas such as the working time directive which sets a maximum working week, if it so chooses. Free market economists will put forward the argument that labour market flexibility will make the UK an attractive location for employers. Weaker employee protection could therefore contribute to job creation. However, some manufacturers and service providers have located in the UK in order to be inside the EU. They may decide to move again, to countries still in the EU.

"Outside of the EU there are two major potential benefits for the UK. One, the ability to pursue lighter and better tailored regulation not possible under EU membership; and two, the ability to strike new trade deals with the rest of the world..." David Davis, June 2016, before his appointment as minister for exiting the EU.

Initially, there will be less regulation outside the EU. Taking the example of restrictive practices and mergers, EU deals such as those which reduce anti-competitive behaviour by Microsoft will probably no longer apply to the UK. Either the UK will have to expand the activities of the CMA to compensate for the lost European dimension, or this area will become less regulated. More broadly, the UK will in future have more independence over decisions on regulation. It seems likely, though not inevitable, that there will be lighter regulation in many areas in future.

Once the UK has left the EU, Parliament will have the power to repeal rulings in areas such as the working time directive which sets a maximum working week.

Exam style question, Paper 3

Airport regulation

Evidence A – The Civil Aviation Authority (CAA)
The CAA is the UK's specialist aviation regulator, responsible for:

- safety standards in the aviation industry.
- consumer choice, value for money, and protection when flying.
- improvements in airlines and airports' environmental performance.
- effective management of security risks.

Service standards and charges are regulated at airports with most market power. This currently applies to Heathrow and Gatwick. Regulation of charges is designed to ensure passengers and others benefit from fair charges and services. Currently, Heathrow landing charges (over £20 per passenger) are capped: increases may rise by RPI – 1.3% per year. Gatwick is allowed increases up to RPI + 1%.

Evidence B – BAA Breakup
Major airports were privatised in the 1980s and transferred to the ownership of BAA. This monopoly of the country's three biggest airports came under fierce criticism from passengers and airlines for failing to deliver a good service for millions of passengers passing through London airports each year.

The CAA referred this problem to the Monopolies and Mergers Commission (now part of the CMA) which required BAA to sell Gatwick and Stansted. Gatwick was sold by BAA in 2009 for £1.5bn to the private equity giant Global Infrastructure Partners (GIP). Michael McGhee, the GIP partner leading the acquisition, said the new owners would "upgrade and modernise Gatwick Airport to transform the experience for both business and leisure passengers."

Simon Calder, travel editor of *The Independent*, said "There is ferocious competition between airlines, but very little between airports... we will ultimately have proper competition between airports." BAA chief executive Colin Matthews was concerned that the proposed remedy "may actually delay the introduction of new runway capacity."

Evidence C – 2016
Both Heathrow and Gatwick are operating at around full capacity. They have competed intensely for permission to open an extra runway, which analysts say is badly needed in the south-east. An Airports Commission report in 2015 favoured an extra runway at Heathrow, which also faces the strongest environmental opposition. A final political decision is still awaited at the time of writing.

Gatwick has reported a trend of improving service and customer satisfaction scores under its new owners. The ASQ independent survey which ranks airports internationally on service and satisfaction had Gatwick in 12th place from 22 large European airports in 2009, with an improvement to 7th place by 2015. Service standards and customer satisfaction have also improved at Heathrow.

Questions
a) Discuss the case for CAA price capping when there is competition between Heathrow and Gatwick. *(8 marks)*

b) Passengers are largely unaware of landing charges, which are paid by airlines. Assess the value of consumers' satisfaction scores as a measure of airport performance. *(10 marks)*

c) Assess the merits of the privatisation of airports. *(12 marks)*

d) Evaluate the suggestion that there is excessive regulation of Heathrow and Gatwick airports. *(20 marks)*

Chapter 9

Market failure in society

Terms to revise: market failure; private, external and social costs and benefits; under- and over-consumption and production; structural unemployment, geographical and occupational immobility.

The right to bear arms

"A well-regulated militia, being necessary to the security of a free State, the right of the people to keep and bear arms, shall not be infringed." – (2nd amendment to US constitution)

"Gun and magazine bans are a total failure. That's been proven every time it's been tried... Law-abiding people should be allowed to own the firearm of their choice. The government has no business dictating what types of firearms good, honest people are allowed to own." – (Donaldjtrump.com)

Gun violence in America is off the chart compared with every other country on the planet. The gun-homicide rate per capita in the US is 30 times that of Britain and Australia, 10 times that of India and four times that of Switzerland... I doubt that anyone seriously thinks we have 30 times as many crazy people as Britain or Australia. But we do have many, many more guns. – (Time.com)

Discussion points

How clearly does the 2nd amendment guarantee Americans the right to bear arms?

Does easier access to weapons entirely explain the higher level of gun violence?

Should it be easier for honest UK citizens to own guns?

Economic theory assumes that the prices people will pay will accurately reflect both the benefit from consumption and the cost of supply. The resulting allocation of resources will give consumers the best available combination of goods and services. Consumers and firms with perfect information act 'rationally'. However these assumptions cannot always be relied upon. In practice the allocation of resources may be sub-optimal because of market failure. There will be over-production and consumption of some things (such as guns) and under-production and consumption of others.

Public goods

There are some situations in which the market cannot work. **Public goods** are non-excludable, meaning that consumption can't be limited to those who pay. So, for example, everyone will benefit if air quality improves. A lighthouse can't turn off its signal because some ships haven't paid a fee. This is sometimes called the 'free rider problem': there is a benefit, but no individual or business has an incentive to provide the public good. The only way to provide it and pay for it is for society as a whole to take responsibility. In practice local and national government provide most public goods using tax revenue.

Free riders

Public goods are also non-rivalrous. Consumption of most goods and services uses them up so less is available for others. But if one individual gains a sense of security from police services, there is nothing to stop others from feeling the same benefit. When drivers are safer on well-lit motorways at night, the same lighting is available for other travellers to use.

Non-rivalrous

Changes in technology can alter the boundaries of what is and is not a public good. Broadcast television signals were once thought of as a public good, both non-rivalrous and non-excludable, but decoders and other technology now make exclusion possible.

Think!
Explain why foreign policy, traffic lights and gun control are provided by governments.

Merit and demerit goods

The key feature of merit goods is that some consumers underestimate their value and so under-consume them. There may be lack of knowledge, called an 'information gap', or people may irrationally ignore available information. Some children underestimate the value of school. If education were provided at cost, some parents wouldn't pay for the education to equip their children for full participation in society. Value judgements are involved: successive governments have judged that providing state education free to age 18 and making attendance compulsory are justified.

Under-consumption

Under-consumption is also likely in the context of health care. If it is not free of charge, some people with serious health problems will not get the care they need because they cannot afford to pay. Health care funded by taxes is available to all on the basis of need and benefits society as a whole.

Over-consumption

Demerit goods are overconsumed in a free market. People underestimate or ignore the negative results of consumption. Uncontrolled access to guns can produce very negative externalities. Tobacco smoking and alcohol threaten the wellbeing of the individual and are costly to society, involving many health problems and sometimes endangering the people around them.

> **Public goods** will not be adequately provided by a free market because the benefits are for all. (They are non-excludable and non-rivalrous.) So they must be provided by society as a whole.
>
> **Merit goods** are under-consumed in a free market either because people underestimate the benefits of consuming them or because they cannot afford to pay for them.
>
> **Demerit goods** are over-consumed by buyers who overestimate their benefits due to information gaps or human irrationality.

Positive and negative externalities

External costs

Merit goods offer external benefits. For example, universal education is an investment in human capital which improves the quality of the working population so the whole community gains. Free health care benefits society by reducing the spread of infectious diseases. Demerit goods have external costs. Think of the costs to the health service of alcohol and tobacco consumption. These externalities make it important for society to provide merit goods and to restrain the use of demerit goods. (See Chapter 10.)

Social benefits

Merit goods are likely to be under-produced as well as under-consumed, if they are not provided by society as a whole and some people cannot pay for them on their own. The social benefits exceed the private benefits of provision.

Demerit goods will be over-produced and over-consumed if the demand for them is not restricted. They are restricted because the social costs (negative externalities) that they create are greater than the private costs.

> **Think!**
> When would health care and education be under-produced and under-consumed? Give examples and explain the possible negative externalities.

Geographical and occupational immobility

Economic theories start from the assumption that when there is creative destruction, factors of production can move easily from one use to another. The land, capital and labour released when an industry declines are transferred to growing sectors. Sometimes this works. At other times there is market failure.

Resource immobility

Farmland could be converted to use for homes, offices or factories. But in practice, the planning system makes permission for conversion to other uses difficult to obtain. Consequently, agricultural land generally sells at prices below £10,000 per acre. Land with planning permission can fetch £200,000 per acre. Conversion is often easier for 'brownfield' sites where previous industrial use has stopped.

Capital equipment such as vehicles, office equipment and buildings can often be transferred from one industry to another. Some capital is difficult to reuse. An obvious example (of a sunk cost) is the investment in shafts and underground equipment for mines. The cost and danger involved in retrieving these things can be prohibitive, so old mines are often sealed up and abandoned. In this case the capital is simply written off. Mobility of capital items is variable.

Occupational immobility

Human capital built up in skills, training and experience also has variable mobility. Mismatches create problems. The decline of manufacturing industries in the UK has reduced demand for many specialist skills, making some obsolete. Mining, shipbuilding and other industries which have declined had highly skilled and specific jobs. Unskilled roles were also lost. There has been extensive structural unemployment where many redundancies occurred. When people cannot learn new skills this is called **occupational immobility**.

Some individuals who have been deskilled by industrial change have been able to rise admirably to the challenge of changing circumstances. Almost 13,000 people have set up new businesses in North West England – an area of high structural unemployment (DWP data). Some of these businesses will thrive. Other unemployed workers have lost income, suffered depression and had various social and health problems. Limited mobility creates human problems at the same time as wasting resources.

Retraining

Flexibility

Governments and businesses can help considerably by providing facilities for retraining. An important social benefit of education is that it can make people more flexible. The concept of lifelong learning has taken hold and does help.

> **Show your understanding**
> Identify two industries or locations where redundancies have caused significant unemployment. Explain why occupational immobility has been problematic for them.

Geographical immobility

Geographical immobility occurs if moving to work in another area is difficult. It is caused by lack of affordable housing in places where labour is in demand. In the north east of England where unemployment is often high, poor public transport limits the distances people can travel to work. Social ties may be another factor, perhaps less significant.

> **Example**
> 'Boomerang generation' is the term for 20-something young adults who stay in the parental home, unable to afford a place of their own. The UK has around 3 million young adults trapped with their parents, unable to fund rents or mortgage payments in major cities. This blocks them from many careers. Perhaps 48% of European 20-somethings now live with parents (*Daily Telegraph*). Young people were once seen as very geographically mobile, but are less so now.

> **Geographical mobility** refers to the ability of workers to move to where jobs are available.
>
> Being able to move from one type of work to another is **occupational mobility**.

House price and rent differentials create big problems for people who need to move to find work. The table shows the most expensive and cheapest cities for the average house early in 2016. Such contrasts prevent geographical mobility.

Moving to a cheaper area allows people the choice of a better house or a smaller mortgage. In reality, a mortgage for a move to London is impossible for many people, and would anyway reduce their standard of living. Lack of geographical and occupational mobility hinders efficient use of labour.

Area	Average price (£)
Greater London	651,013
Cambridge	421,703
Brighton	369,062
Bristol	296,563
Belfast	188,624
Manchester	164,696
Glasgow	168,531
Liverpool	155,965

Source: Zoopla

Find out

Look for the prices of small flats or bedsits available for rent in your area.

How much would you need to earn before you could afford this rent?

How might property prices affect your future career?

Imperfect and asymmetric information

Imperfect information

The assumption that buyers and sellers have perfect information is questionable in many situations. Quite often, both buyer and seller will have imperfect information. Job applications and interviews don't give employers a fully accurate picture about applicants, who themselves might not get a realistic picture of the work. In extreme cases, dishonest dentists have lied to patients in order to get agreement to expensive dental work. In some tourist areas restaurants with cheap menu prices but service charges and expensive drinks entice customers to spend more than they anticipate. These are cases of asymmetric information, with sellers having better information than buyers.

> Buyers and/or sellers who don't know everything about a transaction have **imperfect information**.
>
> **Asymmetric information** occurs if either buyer or seller knows more than the other.
>
> **Information failures** such as these are likely to distort resource allocation.

Over-priced complementary goods

When sellers suggest adding complementary goods to a transaction, they will sometimes hope that convenience will mask poor value. For example, holiday bookers are often offered travel insurance when they book, and some holiday firms make travel insurance compulsory. The price charged is often double the price of travel insurance bought separately. Similarly, many products are offered with extended warranties, which can be poor value. When I bought stickers to refresh the lettering on my battered computer keyboard, one seller offered a bargain price of £2.07, plus the opportunity of a 3 year 'Square Trade' warranty for £8.49. I found that resistible. Nervous buyers of large electrical items are often vulnerable to warranties which offer poor value.

Holiday bookers are often offered travel insurance when they book, and some holiday firms make travel insurance compulsory.

Mis-selling

> **Example**
> Payment Protection Insurance (PPI) is sold as a complement to credit cards and other financial products. In theory, it helps borrowers make repayments even if redundancy or sickness create problems. It has been bundled with new cards and loans, despite having conditions which block many claims. For example, redundancy claims are impossible for the retired or self-employed, yet they were sold PPI. Sales peaked at over 7 million policies per year in 2008, and sellers' made big profits, even though Citizens' Advice had made a super-complaint to the OFT in 2005. In 2011, after court cases, the banks had to pay compensation for mis-selling PPI. Over £20bn had been paid in compensation by mid-2016. Banks had exploited asymmetrical information.

Some second hand cars are sold because they are going wrong. It is difficult for buyers to distinguish between a top quality car and one with an underlying problem. This uncertainty helps to explain the rapid fall in car prices once they leave the showroom. Typically, cars lose up to 40% of their value in their first year and 60% in three years (AA data). Information gaps have a significant impact in this market.

Consequences of environmental change

Environmental changes occur both naturally and as a result of human activity. Climate change involves unpredictable weather systems and more extreme events such as floods and droughts. This brings assorted external costs, some of which are considered in the next chapter. It brings more uncertainty to farmers and to others, making business decisions more difficult and sometimes requiring changes in the allocation of resources.

It is almost impossible to define the precise extent of the damage caused by businesses and governments when their investments and production processes have big carbon footprints. The external costs cannot be quantified: we do not know exactly how much damage they are going to cause. One of the fastest growing sources of carbon emissions is air travel. It would be possible to put an extra 10% tax on all air travel prices. The entire proceeds could be given to research bodies that would invent crafty ways of mitigating the external costs of air travel. So far very few politicians have suggested this.

New technologies

As sea levels rise, coastal land will be flooded more frequently. Many people have argued that new technologies will deal with the problem. Businesses are spending more on research into cleaner products and there is progress. The fall in the price of solar panels is helping.

> **Think!**
> The Zika virus involves both natural and man-made elements to a growing problem. Zika fever is a disease spread mainly by mosquito bites. The direct consequences for most sufferers are generally milder than with malaria. A bigger problem is that children born to infected mothers can suffer serious birth defects, including brain malformation in some cases.
>
> The mosquitos which infect Zika have gradually spread to additional tropical regions. This is partly natural, but aided by globalisation increasing contacts between regions. An epidemic in Central America has been causing concern since 2015. Climate change adds an extra dimension by extending the range in which the mosquitos are active. One research project, for example, has found the mosquitos surviving winter in Washington D.C. Research into both vaccines and eliminating mosquitos has become a high priority and potentially profitable resource use.
>
> Why have many people been rather slow to support action on environmental issues? How might people and businesses be persuaded to take early action on environmental issues?

Research into Zika is a reaction to an increasing problem. In an uncertain world it is hard to successfully anticipate developments and pre-empt problems. Responses to environmental change are often left until there is a major problem, when earlier action could have been preferable.

Exam style question (Section C)

Fracking

Evidence A – Fracking basics

Hydraulic fracturing is a process which involves drilling down into the earth and injecting a high-pressure mixture of water, sand and chemicals to release gas in shale rock. Estimates say there could be as much as 1,300 trillion cubic feet of shale gas under parts of central and northern England. This could provide more than 500 years of gas supply for the UK.

Adapted from gov.uk and Theweek.co.uk

Evidence B – Possible benefits

● Energy security with reduced reliance on imports and perhaps lower prices.

● Creation of up to 74,000 jobs (Institute of Directors estimate).

● Reduced imports so better balance of payments on current account.

● Local communities gain from 1% of revenue earned in their area.

● "Fracking Is Misunderstood, It's The Key To Energy Self-Sufficiency."

Adapted from UKOOG.org and Forbes.com

Evidence C – Possible costs

● Large quantities of water needed for fracking.

● Risk of groundwater contamination and methane gas leaks.

● Risk of earthquakes (mainly minor).

● Extending reliance on climate changing fossil fuels.

● "You can be in favour of fracking, and you can be in favour of tackling climate change, but you can't be in favour of both."

Adapted from newscientist.org and greenpeace.org

Evidence D – Committee on Climate Change (CCC)

The CCC wants three key tests met if fracking is to be approved:

● Strict regulation, monitoring and limiting of emissions.

● No rise in overall gas consumption (just substitution for imports).

● Fracking emissions included in UK carbon 'budget'.

Adapted from gov.uk and Theweek.co.uk

Question

Evaluate the extent to which externalities should influence decisions on fracking.   *(20 marks)*

Chapter 10

Externalities

Terms to revise: all previous work on market failure.

Recycling

The benefits of recycling can include:

Lower costs. Using recycled materials is often cheaper than starting with fresh raw materials.

Resource conservation. Scarce natural resources are depleted less rapidly if items are recycled.

Waste reduction. Less need for landfill and other forms of waste disposal such as burning.

Energy savings. Converting raw resources to usable materials often involves high energy use.

Job creation. More recycling could create 10,000 UK jobs. (*The Guardian*, 11 June 2013.)

Improved balance of payments. Less need to import expensive raw materials.

Healthier environment. Could contribute to slowing climate change, for example.

Discussion points

Which of the list above offer private benefits to recyclers?

Which offer external benefits?

Do the external benefits justify government support for recycling?

Private, external and social costs and benefits

Spillover effects

Economic activity often has 'spillover' effects beyond its impact on the buyers and sellers involved in transactions. Because the benefit or cost of such effects is not included in prices that are paid, these are **external benefits and costs** which the price mechanism doesn't allow for. The example of recycling shows how externalities can be involved in market failure. The cost of recycling is sometimes a little more than using raw materials. A firm guided by market forces would only consider **private costs and benefits** and choose the cheaper option, so not recycle. It is quite possible, though, that the external benefits from using recycled materials would more than compensate for a higher cost. An external benefit is a free gain. It is a situation where one person or a group of people benefit from the actions of others but are not expected to make any payment. In this case, an overall benefit from recycling is ignored by market signals. This is a market failure.

> **External benefits** are benefits affecting anyone other than the buyer or seller, i.e. a third party.
>
> **External costs** are costs which impact on third parties.
>
> **Private costs** are paid by the seller and **private benefits** are the buyer's gain from consumption.

Example

External benefits

Honey producers keep bees in hives, leaving the bees to do most of the work until the owners collect the honey they make. The process entails bees collecting pollen from plants and trees. In most cases, bees wander beyond the producer's premises and visit fields and gardens over some distances. The honey producer gets a benefit from plants and trees which belong to someone else. Because the beekeepers have no costs or responsibility for these plants and trees, they derive an external benefit.

In the context of bees, the flow of external benefits works in both directions. Many fruit and vegetable crops depend on pollination for successful growth. Pollination is most often carried out by bees. When these bees belong to a beekeeper rather than the farmer, or even when bees are wild, farmers gain an external benefit from the service bees provide. Recent diseases amongst bees have made farmers very aware of how much they depend on this benefit.

External costs

Congestion

If a water company finds that an old underground pipe has broken and is leaking badly, they are responsible for fixing it. As many water pipes run under roads, this will often entail closing part or all of a road whilst repairs are made. The costs of the labour, materials and equipment used for the repair will be paid by the water company. There could be other costs generated which they might not have to pay, leaving someone else to cope with them. These are external costs. An obvious example is the cost of congestion and delays which might be caused by road closure. Less obviously, the leaking water could cause damage to nearby property.

Whether or not the water company pays for such damage to property will depend on the legal system. The law would probably allow a property owner to claim the cost of damage from the water company, though it might be necessary to prove that the company had been negligent in allowing the pipe to deteriorate. The legal system does not protect drivers and businesses affected by road closures. Spectacular traffic jams in China in the summer of 2010 included one 75 mile queue and roadworks that caused a backlog of traffic that took nine days to clear. Despite the extent of the external costs imposed on road users, there was no compensation.

Spectacular traffic jams in China in 2010 included one 75 mile queue and roadworks that caused a backlog of traffic that took nine days to clear.

Atmospheric pollution

Increasing attention is now being paid to global external costs arising from the use of fossil fuels, particularly oil. The great majority of scientific opinion accepts that burning fossil fuels is the biggest single contributor to the process of global warming. Atmospheric pollution from fossil fuels also damages crops and buildings. Oil spills during production and transportation add more external costs. No property rights protect us from global warming, and some of the biggest fossil fuel businesses still deny that their activities create the problem. By contrast, after the Deepwater Horizon spill in the Gulf of Mexico, BP was required to set aside $55bn to pay for the clean-up costs, fines, penalties and damages. Most if not all of the external costs were paid for.

When we consider external costs as well as those which are private, we refer to the combined total as **social costs**. Similarly, **social benefits** are the total of private plus any external benefits. From an overall perspective, production is worthwhile if social benefits are greater than social costs. Free markets will often over-produce or under-produce because they ignore externalities.

> **Social costs** are the total of private and external costs from any activity.
>
> **Social benefits** are the total of private and external gains from any activity.

The impact of prices not reflecting social costs

The costs that a supplier will consider, the private costs, determine supply. The private marginal cost curve is the basis for the supply curve. Similarly, private marginal benefits determine the demand curve. The last unit bought and sold should have marginal cost and revenue which just balance. In theory, the quantity where they balance should be allocatively and productively efficient. However, when there are external benefits and/or costs the situation will change. (See Figure 1 overleaf.)

Diagrams illustrate this situation well. The marginal private cost (mpc) curve illustrates private costs. External costs can be added to give the marginal social cost (msc), with the vertical difference between these two curves showing the extent of external costs. The free market output would be Q1 on Figure 1, where marginal cost and benefit cross. However, the social cost is much more than the benefit of the last unit, so making and selling it is a bad choice for overall welfare. Reducing output and sales to Q2, where the social benefits match the social cost, would be the best resource use.

Marginal costs and benefits

Figure 1: External cost

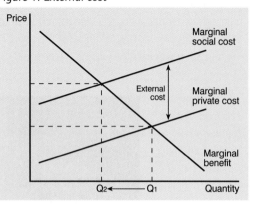

Figure 2: External benefit

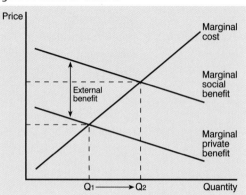

Figure 2 shows external benefits, which a free market would ignore at its equilibrium output of Q1. In this case the marginal social benefit is much more than the marginal cost at Q1 so increasing output up to point Q2 would be desirable. A free market will under-produce where there are external benefits, just as it will over-produce where there are external costs.

Thinking back to the broken water pipe, it will need fixing. Perhaps, though, there will be a choice between fixing it during the working day, at night, or even on a Sunday. Night or Sunday working would involve higher private costs so would not be the selfish choice for the water company. However, the external cost of congestion caused by the repair should be lower at quiet times, so that might be the best option overall.

Valuing externalities

Sometimes external costs (or benefits) can be clearly identified and are quite easy to value. In the case of congestion, it is possible to place a value on extra hours worked and extra fuel used. Subjective valuations and information gaps can make valuing some externalities dependant on guesstimates or simply impossible. Noise pollution is unpleasant but difficult to value. Seeing other people cry can upset many of us, but could we put a value on the external cost of that upset?

Costing the hole in the ozone layer

> There is a hole in the ozone layer above the South Pole. CFC gases released into the atmosphere were held partly responsible. As ozone protects the Earth from harmful UV rays from the sun, the growing hole was bad news. CFC production was phased out by the start of this century. In June, 2016, 'Science' reported that between 2000 and 2014 the hole shrunk by 4 million square miles. It might be closed in around 50 years. This is good news, but it would be difficult to value the net benefit. We could arrive at an estimate of the private costs of switching from CFCs to substitutes, but how could the cost of the ozone layer hole be estimated? Has it played any part in the increased incidence of skin cancers? How much has it contributed to global warming?

We know that ignoring external costs and benefits will result in market forces allocating resources in ways which don't maximise welfare. Sometimes we can accurately identify the extent of the problem and see how much over-production or under-production there is. At other times, we can identify problems but cannot be confident about measuring their extent.

Environmental externalities

Both production and consumption can create external costs that damage the environment. This can be localised, as when a factory releases pollutants in its area or a traffic jam of holidaymakers brings gridlock to roads. It can also be global; climate change has implications for the entire planet.

Think!

Patio heaters burn liquid petroleum gas and radiate heat in their immediate vicinity. They have been estimated to each produce 4 tonnes of CO_2 in a year if used regularly. CO_2 is involved in climate change. Some restaurants and bars find that multiple patio heaters attract extra business in cool weather. Some households extend their barbecue season by using them. An EU proposal to ban patio heaters failed in 2008. One expert said that millions of televisions currently make a bigger contribution to climate change than patio heaters. The DIY chain B&Q stopped selling them in 2013 for environmental reasons, though they were profitable.

1. Explain likely causes of the failure of the EU proposal.

2. What measures might be used to prevent businesses from engaging in polluting activities?

Environmental externalities

The patio heater is relevant to a number of issues around environmental externalities. As a business choice for a bar or restaurant, installing them can add to revenue and profits. Manufacturers, distributors and retailers can also profit. Many people gain pleasure from using them. On the other hand, they release CO_2 and so create external costs by contributing to global warming and climate change.

In 2006, the Stern Review of climate change for the UK government said that *"the evidence gathered by the review leads to a simple conclusion: the benefits of strong and early action far outweigh the economic costs of not acting."* There is still denial that climate change poses a serious threat in some quarters, so the Intergovernmental Panel on Climate Change expresses itself carefully, recently saying that *"Taken as a whole, the range of published evidence indicates that the net damage costs of climate change are likely to be significant and to increase over time."*

Looking at specific consequences of climate change there are serious and growing problems

● Global sea level has risen by about 19 cms. since reliable record keeping began in 1880. It is projected to rise another 30 to 120 centimetres by 2100. This is the result of added water from melting land ice and the expansion of seawater as it warms.

● Human-induced warming is superimposed on a naturally varying climate so the temperature rise has not been, and will not be, uniform or smooth. The incidence of extreme weather events such as flooding and droughts is projected to increase.

● If heat-trapping gas emissions continue to grow, increases of a month or more in the lengths of the frost-free and growing seasons are possible in some regions, whilst other regions will become less fertile and desertification is likely to increase.

Drought problems

These problems will affect different regions in different ways. The government of The Maldives (low lying islands in the Indian Ocean) is searching for new homes for their people. Densely populated low-lying areas of Bangladesh are expected to flood more frequently, with land areas shrinking. In 2016 Ethiopia is suffering its worst drought in 50 years. Successive 'rainy seasons' have failed to arrive; the drought has killed up to 90% of crops in some areas and at least one million cattle. Developed countries are not immune. California and much of Australia have serious drought problems. There has been an impact on plant and animal species in Europe (with some pests reaching new areas) as well as more flooding and water shortages in parts of the continent.

The impact and the external costs involved vary from area to area, but bring a *"fundamental threat to places, species and people's livelihoods"* (WWF). Attempting to value the costs would be difficult. Similarly, apportioning responsibility would be extremely complex. It is widely accepted, though, that greenhouse gases such as CO_2 are the main cause and that many emissions result from the use of fossil fuels such as coal, oil and gas. Besides global warming, there are other more measurable impacts.

Rapid development in China has resulted in pollution and persistent smog in industrialised areas. The World Bank reported that *"hundreds of thousands of premature deaths and incidents of serious respiratory illness [have been] caused by exposure to industrial air pollution. Seriously contaminated by industrial discharges, many of China's waterways are largely unfit for direct human use."* As one example, fine particles from vehicle exhausts can cause asthma, bronchitis, and acute and chronic respiratory symptoms and may be linked to lung cancer.

Gainers and losers

Awareness of such issues has grown in China; there were some reductions in emissions in 2016. There is also growing determination to tackle environmental damage around the world, though progress is generally slow. The fundamental problem in most places is that, as with patio heaters, the external costs to the environment are to entire communities whilst measures to reduce them disadvantage groups whose livelihoods and profits depend on polluting activities.

Exam style question (Paper 3)

Overfishing

Evidence A – Fishing technology

Successive technological developments have made fishing fleets more efficient. Examples include:

- Fibre technology improving net design, weight and construction.

- Computer aided vessel and gear design improving performance and efficiency.

- Sonar and GPS technology to precisely locate shoals of fish.

- Processing and refrigeration technology enabling fleets to stay at sea for longer.

Adapted from FAO.org

Evidence B – Unsustainable fishing

- If fish are caught at a faster rate than they can reproduce, the stock of fish will decline.

- The global fishing fleet is 2-3 times larger than the level which oceans can sustainably support.

- WWF estimate that 53% of fisheries are fully exploited and 32% are overexploited.

- Several major commercial fish populations have declined to the point where their survival is uncertain. Without improvement, all species fished for food are predicted to collapse by 2048.

Adapted from WWF.org

Evidence C – The Grand Banks

Cod fisheries at The Grand Banks off Newfoundland supported the largest fishery in the world. Fishing boomed in the 1970s and 1980s, with 10,000 fishermen and 30,000 related jobs dependent on fishing. In 1992, overfishing left cod stocks exhausted and the industry collapsed. The Canadian government introduced a total ban on cod fishing. There has been some recovery in the last 10 years, but there are still insufficient cod stocks in the area to make a major fishery viable again.

Adapted from youtube.com and NewScientist.com

Evidence D – The tragedy of the Commons

In the past, many towns and villages had 'commons', areas of land on which anyone could graze animals. In 1832, an early economist noted that the quality of grazing on commons was consistently poorer than on privately owned land. Adding extra animals on the common brought a short term profit for their owner, whilst overgrazing disadvantaged everyone in the long run. If one person reduced their number of animals, other people might just add more.

Adapted from youtube.com

Questions

a) Discuss the relevance of 'the tragedy of the commons' to the Grand Banks fishery.   *(8 marks)*

b) Assess the contribution of technological change to overfishing.   *(10 marks)*

c) Assess the likely external benefits to Newfoundland from the earlier flourishing fishery.   *(12 marks)*

d) Evaluate the suggestion that external costs arising from overfishing will cause all commercial fisheries to collapse.   *(20 marks)*

Chapter 11

Policies to deal with market failure

Plastic bags

8.5bn plastic bags were given to customers by UK supermarkets in 2014. They are low cost and convenient to use. Many carried a brand name or logo which benefitted the store by bringing them to the attention of passers-by. These bags had become a fixture in the UK shopping experience as in many other countries.

Plastic bags, used on average for 12 minutes, can take 1,000 years to degrade and cause many problems. Seabirds and fish suffer from ingesting plastic which can block the gut and prove fatal. At sea and onshore, the build-up of plastic bag litter was "an iconic symbol of waste" (Defra). Plastic bags are clearly a demerit good.

In October, 2015, the UK government introduced a 5p levy for single use plastic bags. There were minor problems with thefts from self-checkouts and spillages from juggling too many purchases, but the scheme is working. Consumers have adjusted, bag use is down by around 80% and most of the levy collected has been given to good causes.

Discussion points

Why was a levy introduced?

Put forward reasons why a charge of just 5p reduced bag use by 80%.

How should the lasting success or failure of the levy be measured?

Public and merit goods

Public sector provision

Free markets will not produce public goods. Non-excludability and the free rider problem mean that a supplier would struggle to collect revenue, even if the product created very desirable benefits. The non-rivalrous nature of public goods is also unusual. The traditional solution, which helps to explain the name of public goods, was to fund and arrange supply in the public sector. So, for example, the protections of police and defence forces are directly provided by the state in almost all countries.

Free markets will produce merit goods, but not normally in desirable quantities. Provision of services such as state education and healthcare can be made in the public sector. This is often found alongside private sector provision for those who choose this option.

High cost

There has been dissatisfaction with direct public provision. The absence of competition and market signals brings a risk of X-inefficiency (page 12) and so productive inefficiency. Without supply and demand to determine equilibrium quantity, there could be over-provision or under-provision and so allocative inefficiency. A third problem is that provision can be very expensive, taking a large share of public sector spending and pushing politicians to raise taxes.

Privatisation

One reaction to these perceived problems has been to privatise ancillary activities whilst keeping core services in the public sector. So, for example, cleaning and catering have been privatised across most of the public sector. NHS trusts can now buy some treatments from the private sector, blurring the boundary between core and ancillary services. The Kings Fund, which researches health care issues, says less than 10% of all treatment is currently bought from private providers. Both health trusts and public opinion are wary about extending privatisation into NHS treatments.

Many public and merit goods are largely taken for granted today. Changes occur but at the margins. Basic provision, developed since the industrial revolution, has greatly improved the quality of life for all, creating civilised solutions to many problems. That said, there are instances of government failure and there is always considerable room for improvement.

Since 1992, many major investments such as in schools, hospitals and prisons have been made through public-private partnerships such as Private Finance Initiatives.

Funding public and merit goods

Private Finance Initiative

Since 1992, many major investments such as in schools, hospitals and prisons have been made through public-private partnerships such as Private Finance Initiatives (PFI). Initial funding and construction is by the private sector. A short term gain is that costs are initially kept off public sector accounts. Private constructors have market pressure to work efficiently and limit costs to make profit, so might be less wasteful. In theory, business risk is also transferred to the private sector.

PFI schemes have attracted criticism. Users such as NHS trusts repay the PFI operators, for up to 25-30 years. Limited competition, asymmetric information and very detailed contracts obscure the costs. PFIs may drain money from public sector budgets. Cathy Newman of Channel 4 FactCheck said *"What started as a neat idea to get big business to help fund public building schemes has ended up allowing some in the private sector to enrich themselves at the expense of the state."*

Table 1: Benefits and costs of PFI

Benefits of PFI	Disadvantages of PFI
Initial funding shifted from public sector	Expensive ongoing repayments
Efficient private sector construction	Risk of 'cutting corners' to boost profit
Risk transferred to private sector	Public sector really covers most risk

Example

Two Coventry hospitals were to have been renovated by the public sector for £30m. Instead they were demolished and a PFI scheme provided a £410m replacement. The NHS trust had to borrow £54m to make its first payment to the consortium. Jonathan Fielden, chair of the British Medical Association's consultants' committee, said that the trust was forced to mothball services and close wards as it could no longer afford to run all the services it had commissioned. (*The Guardian*)

In total the UK owes more than £222bn to banks and businesses as a result of PFIs (*The Independent on Sunday*). The gains from PFI, other than shifting the initial costs to the private sector, have sometimes seemed uncertain. One of the strongest criticisms, in *The Guardian*, saw PFI "As a tangible symbol of rip-off Britain and the failed privatisation of the public sector." Partnership between the public and private sectors has not always been successful.

> **Think!**
> An alternative way of funding public and merit goods would be a tax increase. Consider the pros and cons of both approaches.

Indirect taxes and subsidies

Merit goods and products with externalities have free market price signals which fail to accurately reflect the full social costs and benefits involved. One policy option for governments is to use taxes and subsidies

Figure 1: Indirect tax to offset external costs

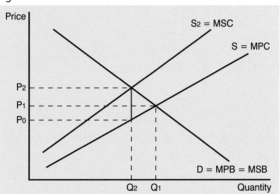

to push prices and quantities closer to the optimum position. Where there are external costs, a tax to increase the price and so reduce consumption could bring sales closer to the point where social costs and benefits are balanced. In the diagram alongside, a free market would produce Q_1, whereas Q_2 is the social optimum. Adding a tax equal to the vertical red line (from P_0 to P_2) could push sales and consumption back to Q_2.

MSC includes private and external costs

The three main excise duties are on products with external costs: alcoholic drink, tobacco and petrol/diesel. In mid-2016, the duty rate was around £3.50 on 20 cigarettes, 50p on a pint of beer, £11 on a bottle of spirits and 58p per litre of petrol. In all these cases, VAT is also charged on the price including duty, so the total tax paid is higher. For example, the Tobacco Manufacturers Association estimates that total tax on 20 premium cigarettes is £6.91. (See Figure 1, page 54 to help interpret this.)

> **Find out!**
> These tax rates change relatively frequently.
> Research the current prices of cigarettes, drink and petrol.
> How much of the current prices of these items is excise duty and how much is the total tax?

Assess the case for levying excise taxes

Tobacco, alcohol and petrol all have price inelastic demand. Low PED means that high tax rates are needed to reduce consumption, and that their tax revenue makes a major contribution to public sector income.

Whether these excise duties reduce sales to the point where social cost and social benefit balance is difficult to know. Estimates of the external costs involved tend to vary.

Subsidies

Where there are merit goods and external benefits, subsidies can be used to shift supply curves downwards, reduce price and so increase consumption. One contributor to lower CO_2 emissions is renewable energy. So, for example, subsidies were offered for the installation of solar panels.

**Controlling
CO2 emissions**

Tradable pollution permits

A more direct way to restrict CO_2 emissions is via tradable permits. If an authority decides a quantity of emissions to allow, which is often less than previous levels, permits for the allowed quantity can be issued to businesses which emit CO_2. This can force them to reduce emissions. Firms which succeed in reducing emissions to below the level they have permits for will have spare permits to sell at auction.

Firms which struggle to reduce emissions might need to buy extra permits. The market will set a price for spare permits, giving a financial reward to firms which reduce emissions most and so have more to sell. Emitting more will prove expensive and so be discouraged. The practical difficulties in allocating permits and monitoring emissions mean that systems might operate less than perfectly. However, permit schemes can make a real contribution to cutting external costs.

> **Example**
> The first large scale tradable permit scheme was the EU Emissions Trading Scheme (EU ETS), which started operating in 2005. Systems were refined during the early phases and the scheme has evolved. By 2010 it was claimed that emissions had fallen by 8% since 2005. Proposed caps for 2020 represented a 21% reduction from 2005 levels. This target was reached 6 years early in 2014. Brexit will move the UK out of EU ETS, and the UK government will decide on any future national controls.

**Keeping
people
informed
of the facts**

Public information

The most direct way of addressing information failures and gaps is to publish information. UK governments have often used printed information, film and advertisements to spread messages which address information gaps or misinformation. Encouraging us to eat our '5 a day', for example, is one of many public health messages. In October, 2012, 41,000 pages of content from 10 government department websites were reformatted when Gov.uk became the main interface for public information.

Public information campaigns can educate, inform and improve decision making. Ten areas in which successes have been claimed are: vaccinations, vehicle safety, safer workplaces, control of infectious diseases, decline in heart attacks and strokes, safer and healthier foods, healthier mothers and babies, family planning, fluoridation of drinking water and recognition of the dangers in tobacco.

> **Try this**
> Have a look at https://www.youtube.com/watch?v=m0xmSV6aq0g or similar sites which show public information films from previous decades. Some of them are as scary as Hollywood B movies.

Campaigns are not all successful. An official pre-referendum pamphlet of information on the EU was regarded as biased in some quarters and might well have been counterproductive.

Legislation and regulation

Besides attempting to tweak market forces or to improve information, governments can use legislation and regulation to ban or enforce items and behaviours. Merit items such as seat belts are compulsory and demerit goods such as 'recreational' opiate drugs are banned. Most people obey most laws and regulations for most of the time, so legislation has a real impact on behaviour. The 5p charge on plastic bags in the case study on page 57 is a good example of how charging can reduce the use of a demerit good.

There are likely to be individuals with specific objections to almost any rule or law, and there are broader concerns from some groups about erosion of civil liberties and increases in 'nanny state' intrusion in people's lives. The basic issue here is that we have the right to be silly in many ways but setting limits to the damage we can do, both to others and to ourselves, makes sense to most of us.

In democracies, authorities must retain a consensus for much of what they do if they wish to retain power. Pages 43-4 identified a view that EU regulation had become excessive. This could be a significant factor in the UK departure from the EU. Very often, laws and regulations are intended to compensate for failings of the free market system linked to externalities, merit and demerit goods, information gaps and irrational behaviour. Less regulation can entail accepting more consequences of market failures.

The impact of policies

Addressing market failure

The extent to which free markets fail explains why authorities take many actions intended to improve the performance of the economy and the quality of life. The public sector uses resources in shaping and enforcing policy; measures often also have resource implications for firms and/or for households. This resource cost is only justified if the outcome brings effective improvements.

There is a danger that action can be taken which is ineffective or even counterproductive. In addition, many measures will favour some interest groups whilst disadvantaging others, so authorities have the task of balancing out opposing interests.

Gainers and losers

> **Try this**
> In 1993 a 'fuel price escalator' was introduced in the UK, intended to raise petrol and diesel duties at 3%, 5% and then 6% above the rate of inflation. The intention was to slow the rate of environmental damage from vehicles, reduce congestion and encourage development of cleaner fuels. Rising oil prices compounded the price increases caused by the escalator, and made it very unpopular with hauliers and other road users. In 2000 the tax was only increased in line with inflation. In 2011 the escalator was suspended and duty was cut by 1p. Despite the substantial fall in oil prices from 2014, the escalator has not been reintroduced.
>
> Who were the winners and losers from the oil price escalator?
>
> Should the escalator be reintroduced?

Short term losses vs. long term gains

When authorities take action which produces a net loss in welfare, for example by moving markets further away from the socially ideal level of production and sales, there is government failure. Judgements on what constitutes government failure are often made on a subjective basis, perhaps reflecting the interests of complaining groups but not always the interests of wider society. One of the hardest judgements is of how much action governments should take now to benefit future generations. The desire to win elections makes it difficult for politicians to take a long term view.

> **Exam style question (Paper 3)**
>
> **Cigarette packaging**
>
> **Evidence A – Change in Regulation**
> In March 2015, MPs voted in favour of plain, standard cigarette packs by 367 to 113.
>
> Plain standardised packaging means all cigarette and hand-rolling tobacco packs will look the same. They will have a standard shape without marketing and design features:
>
> ● Picture health warnings will remain.
>
> ● Brand names will be in a standard colour and size.
>
> ● The shape and colour of the packs and cigarettes will be standardised.
>
> ● A 'duty paid' stamp will show the pack is not counterfeit.
>
> Source: Adapted from gov.uk and cancerresearch.org
>
> **Evidence B – Support for the change**
> Smoking is the number one cause of preventable early death. Currently approximately 100,000 people die prematurely from smoking-related diseases every year in the UK. Tobacco companies therefore need to recruit new smokers to stay in business. New customers are nearly always children and young people. Two thirds (66%) of regular smokers started before the age of eighteen – the

legal minimum age for the purchase of tobacco – and two fifths (39%) started before the age of sixteen. Of those who take up smoking, only about half will manage to stop before they die. With other forms of advertising closed to them, tobacco companies have invested a fortune in innovative packaging, creating 'mobile billboards' that appeal to young people.

Australia was the first country to require cigarettes to be sold in plain, standardised packaging. The United Kingdom was the first country in Europe to pass similar legislation, followed by Ireland and France.

Evidence shows that removing all branding and design increases the prominence of warnings on packs and makes cigarettes less attractive to adults and children. This will help prevent young people from taking up smoking and ultimately save lives. This was a big move towards our goal of a tobacco-free generation. Standard packs make health warnings more effective and make the packaging less misleading about the harms of smoking.

Source: Adapted from ASH.org.uk

Evidence C – Opposition

Some people think that the colours, designs and trademarks used on cigarette packs make them more appealing, particularly to young people. However, there is no compelling evidence to suggest that plain packs are effective in discouraging young people from smoking, encouraging existing smokers to quit, or preventing quitters from taking up smoking again. The evidence from Australia shows that plain packaging is not achieving its public health goals – smoking rates have not deviated from historic trends. There has, however, been a significant increase in the size of the illegal tobacco market – the criminals behind this illegal trade are now profiting at the expense of Australian taxpayers, with the Government losing around AUS\$1.42 billion in tax revenue annually. We also consider plain packaging to be unlawful. It involves governments taking property from businesses, in this case our trademarks and other intellectual property. That is illegal under the laws of many countries around the world. A properly functioning consumer goods market relies on having clearly differentiated brands with different quality and price positioning. These differentiating features are all provided by brand trademarks, which enable existing adult smokers to differentiate between brands. Trademarks and branding also provide quality assurance for consumers and retailers – plain packaging removes this assurance.

Source: Adapted from BAT.com

Evidence D – Smoking in decline
Percentage of the UK population who smoke cigarettes, by age group

Year	Age 16-19	20-24	25-34	35-49	50-59	60+
1978	34	44	45	45	45	30
1998	31	40	35	31	28	16
2012	15	29	27	23	21	13

Source: ONS

Questions

a) Referring to the evidence, discuss the importance of packaging in marketing. *(8 marks)*

b) Assess the likelihood of regulation of markets such as tobacco causing illegal activity. *(10 marks)*

c) Assess two possible reasons for the decline in smoking shown in Evidence D. *(12 marks)*

d) Evaluate the decision to impose plain packaging for tobacco products. *(20 marks)*

Chapter 12

The AD/AS model

Terms to revise: aggregate supply and demand, the circular flow of money, injections and leakages, investment, capacity utilisation, government objectives, the economic cycle, productive capacity, demand-pull and cost-push inflation, types of unemployment, contractionary and expansionary policies.

Aston Martin's investment plans

In February 2016 Aston Martin announced that it will build its new DBX in a brand new facility in St. Athan in the Vale of Glamorgan in Wales at a cost of £200m. This is a major coup for Wales; it took two years to secure the deal ahead of 20 locations around the world. Construction will begin in 2017; cars will begin rolling off the production line in 2020.

To survive at the luxury end of the market, the company has been looking at broadening its range to appeal to younger customers, especially women. The car, which is an all-electric 4x4, is expected to cost £160,000 and was unveiled at the Geneva Motor Show in 2015. The CEO said the company envisaged a world "…when luxury travel is not only stylish and luxurious but also more practical, family friendly and environmentally responsible."

The company has also announced a partnership with LeEco, the Chinese backer of the electric car start-up company Faraday Future. They hope to develop the RapidE concept vehicle and think there is the potential to make other cars in the future. Faraday has announced plans to build a production facility in Las Vegas. Aston Martin, despite a century of experience in developing performance cars, is behind the game compared to companies like Ford and Nissan when it comes to producing electric vehicles.

The Chinese government has said it wants five million electric vehicles on its roads by 2020, and is trying to offer incentives to drivers such as exemption from the law that says non-electric vehicles can only be driven on Beijing's roads six days a week. This joint venture intends to bring the RapidE to market by 2018.

Discussion points

Consider the effects of this development on the local area, both positive and negative.

What possible difficulties might Aston Martin encounter?

Aggregate demand

Aggregate demand represents the total level of demand in an economy. It has five components, consumption, investment, government spending, exports and imports. The formula is:

$$AD = C + I + G + (X - M)$$

Consumption is the biggest driver of UK aggregate demand at around 65%, followed by government spending (20%) and investment (18%). Because the UK economy usually has a balance of payments deficit the difference between exports and imports is negative (approx. -3%).

Think!

Successive UK governments have talked about the danger of relying on consumption to fuel our economy, rather than investment or exports. Free market economists do not like leaving economic growth to government spending. You may have read about the initiatives to try and *rebalance* the economy away from consumption and towards investment. How might this help the economy in the short and long run?

In the case study, the first change to aggregate demand comes from Aston Martin's £200m investment in the new factory. This investment creates jobs, not just in the factory but also in the locality and supplier companies. These jobs will reduce unemployment, raise income and increase consumption. As a result of increased AD, income tax and VAT will rise, plus corporation tax if the venture proves profitable. There is

Rising AD

no guarantee that government spending will increase, but it might. Finally if the company needs to buy raw materials from abroad then imports will rise, but hopefully this will be offset by exports, which may rise by a greater amount. The sum total will be an increase in aggregate demand. In a diagram you would show AD shifting to the right.

Watch out!
You can show judgement in examinations by stating that the size of the shift in aggregate demand depends on the scale of the changes taking place. Make sure you have revised the diagram for aggregate demand and supply.

The table below shows the component parts of aggregate demand and the factors that contribute to each one of them.

Component	Affected by
Consumption	● Consumer confidence ● Wage levels ● Interest rates ● Levels of personal taxation ● Levels of employment and unemployment
Investment	● Capacity utilisation ● Confidence ● Interest rates ● Levels of corporation tax
Government Spending	● Government priorities and macro-economic objectives ● Stage in the economic cycle
Imports/Exports	● Exchange rates ● International competitiveness ● State of the global economy

Changes in Aggregate Supply (AS)

Figure 1: Aggregate supply and a rise in demand

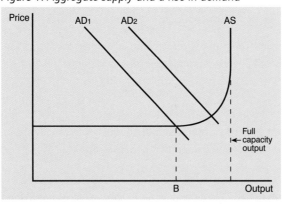

Movement along the AS curve

Skill shortages

Just as aggregate demand measures the level of demand in the whole economy, aggregate supply measures the total output from all activities. Figure 1 shows how output can expand without any increase in prices so long as there are resources available for use (up to AD1 and point B). There is a movement along the AS curve. As output increases, more people are employed. Underutilised capacity is used to expand output. However, at some point, the supply of potential employees with the skills required by the employers will diminish. **Skill shortages** will cause employers to raise pay in order to attract the people they want. This increases costs and prices will rise. With strong demand, it will be possible to produce more and sell the product at a higher price. These conditions indicate a developing boom.

As businesses strive to produce more, prices will rise further, until many **supply constraints** develop. Employees will be working overtime or shifts (night work), for higher pay. Other inputs may become scarce. Machinery may be overloaded. Output will draw closer and closer to its **full capacity** level. This is the absolute maximum that can be produced, given available resources. But growth at this speed is not sustainable.

With strong economic growth, the economy can literally run out of resources to produce more.

Supply constraints

> **Skill shortages**: even when there is some unemployment there may be shortages of people who are available for work and have the skills that are required. Employers may offer higher pay to attract skilled people to move from other jobs.
>
> **Supply constraints** (bottlenecks) include skill shortages but also other constraints such as overloaded infrastructure. Capital investment cannot grow fast enough to keep up with demand.
>
> **Full capacity output** is the maximum level to which aggregate supply can grow.

Full capacity output

Every economy faces the question of how to organise factors of production of land, labour, capital and enterprise. It is helpful to think of enterprise as the skill of organising the other factors of production to produce goods and services which satisfy aggregate demand at a price which is acceptable to both producers and consumers. If all of these factors are organised effectively and demand is sufficient to meet this level of output, the economy will be operating close to full capacity. Below this level of output the economy has under-utilised resources, i.e. spare capacity. In Figure 1, with aggregate demand at AD2, the economy is getting close to full capacity output. Further economic growth is not possible unless the productive potential of the economy is increased. At this level of output any further increase in aggregate

Inflation

demand will be accompanied by **accelerating inflation**. The economy is overheating. Contractionary policies might be implemented and a descent into recession may follow.

> **Accelerating inflation** occurs when the economy is nearing full capacity output. Increased demand for labour (especially for people with scarce skills) means that employers start to raise pay so that they can get the employees they need. This pushes up costs and prices, leading to a wage-price spiral. This occurred in the late 1980s and many times before that.

All this is about what happens in the short run. With strong economic growth, the economy can literally run out of resources to produce more. But in the long run, given time, full capacity output can be increased. Higher investment, training more people so that skills are less scarce, improving training so that employees become more versatile, doing more R&D so that efficiency increases, all help to increase potential output. Better management can, over time, increase productivity. Recruiting people from overseas works too. But these developments take time.

Figure 2: AS in the long run

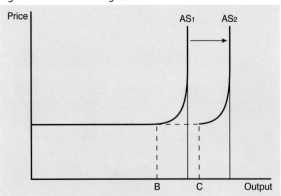

Figure 2 shows how in the long run, full capacity output can grow – shifting from AS1 to AS2. With rapid growth and AD shifting to the right, inflation starts to accelerate at point B because supply constraints are developing. With the extra capacity shown by AS2, output can rise to point C without price rises. With investment, human capital and new technologies, the economy can grow in a way that does not threaten stability. Figure 3 illustrates this.

Figure 3: Rising AD with long term growth in capacity

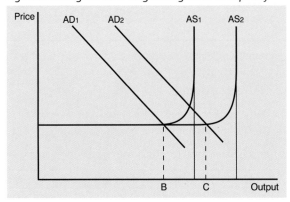

If aggregate demand grows fast, inflation will develop before there is time to increase aggregate supply sufficiently. There will be bottlenecks and cost increases that make price increases inevitable. You can use the AS/AD diagrams to show this. From the policy point of view it is important not to let AD grow unsustainably fast.

> **Show your understanding**
> The Aston Martin story provides a single example of how aggregate demand might rise if a number of businesses are expanding. Draw an AS/AD diagram that indicates what will happen if a number of businesses are investing and growing, in the economy as it is when you are reading this. Think carefully about how you draw the diagram and explain why you have drawn it the way you have.

AD, AS and inflation – the impact of change

Inflation can be defined as a persistent rise in prices across the economy or conversely a fall in the purchasing power of money. Essentially inflation can be caused either by changes in the level of aggregate demand in the economy (demand-pull inflation) or by changes in the costs of production (cost-push inflation). Going back to Figure 1, you can see the effect on the price level of an increase in one or more of the components of aggregate demand. Increased consumption, investment, government spending or exports have shifted AD to the right. Suppliers will react to this increase in demand if they are confident of achieving a price level that makes an increase in production worthwhile. This is demand-pull inflation. Aggregate demand is growing but aggregate supply cannot grow fast enough to meet the demand.

Commodity prices

Figure 4: Cost-push inflation

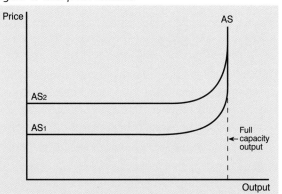

Figure 4 shows the effect of cost-push inflation. Here costs of production have risen and firms have to decide whether to accept a lower level of profit at the same selling price, or whether to raise the price to maintain the same level of profit. This situation is interesting historically because it shows how the AS curve changes when oil or commodity prices rise sharply, as they did in the 1970s and '80s. Essentially, cost-push inflation means that whatever the level of AD, costs and prices will be higher.

In recent years inflation has not been a big problem. Since the mid-1990s, inflation has fluctuated but mostly been below 4% and often around 2%, the target rate. In 2015-16 rates of inflation were so low that there were fears of deflation. This can actually depress economic activity. That is why the Bank of England inflation target is set at 2% per year. (More on that in Chapter 18). However, higher inflation could return, especially if the exchange rate falls.

Oil price fall

Show your understanding

Oil prices were high for some years up to 2013; petrol was around 130p per litre. In 2014 prices began to fall and by early 2016 they were around 100p per litre. With reference to Figure 4, draw your own diagram to show how the oil price fall affected the AS curve, and add an appropriate AD curve. Show the effect of the change in the AS curve on the level of output and how this affected inflation rates. Explain the impact of the oil price fall on individuals and the economy as a whole.

Employment

Expansionary policies

When aggregate demand is very low, many people will be unemployed. There will be much underutilised capacity: output will be well below full capacity. If expansionary policies are employed, consumer spending will rise and the AD curve will shift to the right. Businesses will take on more labour so they can expand output. If the increased demand looks likely to continue, businesses may want to increase investment. Unemployment will fall further. This situation is covered in detail in the next chapter.

On the other hand, increasing use of new technologies may mean that firms can produce more for the same price. AS will be shifting to the right. This could also mean that less labour is demanded (as firms become more capital intensive). If this happen on a large scale, demand for labour might actually fall, creating structural unemployment. It is possible for AS to be growing faster then AD, in which case demand-deficiency unemployment will rise too. This may have happened in the period 2009-12.

Show your understanding

For each of the following changes, explain whether they will affect the demand-side of the economy, the supply-side, or both. Draw diagrams where appropriate.

a) An increase in the rate of income tax.

b) An increase in the minimum wage.

c) Cuts in government expenditure.

d) A spike in world oil prices.

e) A recession in a major export destination.

f) A fall in consumer confidence.

g) Increasing use of robots.

Frictional unemployment

Producing at full capacity does not mean zero unemployment. Every economy needs a certain level of unemployment to allow for changes in the structure of the economy, movement between jobs, and changes in the wage rate. This is frictional unemployment. If the economy is overheating, even frictional unemployment will fall but this will be indicative of unsustainable growth.

Injections

The multiplier

John Maynard Keynes, the economist, pointed out that certain types of spending create multiplier effects. For example, if the UK government increases spending on education by £1 million, the effect will be to increase income for some households (the new teachers employed, the builders etc.) Some of that income will be saved, some taken in tax, and some spent on imported goods. However, the remainder will be spent within the domestic economy. This spending effectively becomes someone else's increased income; they will be able to spend more. This ripple effect continues throughout the economy, triggering further income generation and spending. The net result is that output should increase by more than the initial injection of expenditure.

Infrastructure

Example
Leading investment management company Rathbones suggested in 2016 that UK economic performance is wavering. Edward Smith, strategist at Rathbones, said that government spending on large scale infrastructure projects could be the key to bolstering the UK economy. He said *"There is a wealth of literature to suggest that the fiscal multiplier of infrastructure spending – i.e. its effect on total output – is very substantial, especially when higher spending is not offset by tighter monetary policy."* He went on to say that ideally, from a growth perspective, infrastructure spending should not be accompanied by higher taxation elsewhere.

Leakages

This sequence of events can be triggered by any increase in injections. (Similarly, an increase in leakages will have the reverse effect, leading to lower output or very slow growth.) The flow chart starts with an increase in investment but the outcome would be similar if there were increased government expenditure or tax cuts. A relatively small increase in spending will generate further spending on many goods and services and help the economy to expand. Increasing confidence will encourage many businesses to invest.

| Investment rises | AD up | Employment rises | Incomes rise | Consumption rises | AD up | Employment rises |

> **The Multiplier** represents the size of the **change** in the **level** of economic activity in relation to the original **change** in the level of **expenditure**.

Determining the actual impact of the multiplier is not easy. For people on low incomes, a rise in disposable income may all be spent. Someone on a higher income may save the extra money. As the income generated goes around the circular flow, at each stage some of it will leak away into savings, tax and imports.

Lower government expenditure

As with most economic theories, assumptions are based on the best data available. Until the credit crunch of 2008-9, it was assumed that the multiplier for government spending was fairly small. Lower government spending would not significantly depress GDP. The then Chancellor of the Exchequer, George Osborne, wanted to reduce the government deficit, and suggested that the effect on the economy of government expenditure cuts would be less than the original cut. However in 2012 the IMF (International Monetary Fund) said that during the recession and recovery the true value of the multiplier was between 0.9 and 1.7, much greater than the Chancellor's estimate. The implication was that the cuts did slow down the economy.

How the AS/AD model sheds light on the economy as a whole

The AS/AD model helps us to analyse the impact of many different changes on incomes, output, employment and inflation. It embodies the effects of technological change. But in practice, many other variables can create changes in the economy, including:

Globalisation

● Globalisation has increased competition, helping to reduce inflation but also creating major structural changes.

● Business expectations affect levels of investment (uncertainty may make investors very cautious).

● Changes in income distribution influence the impact of economic change.

● Leaving the EU will lead to significant changes in trade patterns.

Recession

Examining events since 2008 illustrates this. The road to recovery following the global recession of 2008/2009 was long and slow. Joe Grice, Chief Economist at the ONS, said *"It remains the sharpest downturn and slowest recovery on record."* During the financial crisis, the UK economy shrank by 6%; it took six years for the country to recover. Aggregate demand and supply can be used to explore these events.

Pre-2008 the UK economy was growing, albeit slowly, but inflation was under control and there was capacity to grow further. When the recession hit, output fell; aggregate demand contracted to AD2 in Figure 5. There was a reduction in the size of the economy from Y1 to Y2. This was the initial effect of the recession. There had never been a recession against a backdrop of increased globalisation, where the actions of one country significantly affected the performance of another. So where was the trigger for recovery going to come from?

Figure 5: The 2009-12 recession

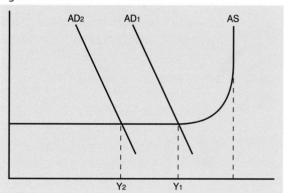

Consumption, the biggest component of AD, was slow to increase. Rising unemployment reduced disposable income. Lack of confidence in the economy slowed consumer purchases and there was no incentive to invest, despite the cost of borrowing being at a record low. The public sector deficit was high because of the cost of rescuing the banks, so the government tried to reduce public expenditure. The slowdown in global trade meant that exports fell. With none of the components of aggregate demand showing signs of growth, the economy was unlikely to recover quickly. As of 2016, the manufacturing sector is still growing slowly but GDP is higher than in 2008, mainly due to growth in services, including finance. The rest of this book explores aspects of this situation.

Exam style question

Rising costs
One month after the 2016 referendum, the boss of Easyjet, Carolyn McCall, told the BBC that its costs had increased by £40m because of the fall in the pound, a consequence of Britain's vote to leave the EU. Easyjet pays for its fuel in US dollars: the 10% fall in the exchange rate raised costs.

The devaluation of the pound since the Brexit vote has also had an impact on 'consumer confidence', or whether people feel compelled to book flights and holidays, she continued. Bookings were down, but she went on to say "It is worth pointing out that although every airline is having a tough time, it is very good news for passengers. It actually means it's cheaper to fly and ticket prices are low."

Using an AD/AS diagram, outline the potential impacts of a weakening pound on the UK economy as a whole. Refer to the passage above and to the content of this chapter. *(20 marks)*

Chapter 13

Demand-side policies

Terms to revise: macroeconomic objectives, fiscal and monetary policy, economic growth, supply constraints, austerity, free market and interventionist policies, policy conflicts and all the terms needed for Chapter 12. (Most of these were outlined in Theme 2.)

Recession

After the financial crisis of 2008-09, the economy went into recession. This was not a surprise – banks stopped lending and this in turn slowed up activity at many businesses and created a downward multiplier.

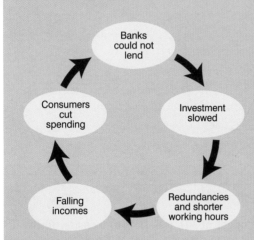

The flow chart shows the sequence of events when the economy went into recession. UK unemployment did not rise nearly so much as it had in previous recessions (1981-84 and 1989-92). Many employers wanted to hang on to their employees, especially those with scarce skills. Instead of making them redundant they reduced their hours; many people also took a pay cut in order to keep their jobs.

The government did not cut spending because that would have reduced aggregate demand still more. But its tax revenues shrank as incomes fell and jobs became harder to find. The public sector deficit increased.

Discussion point

What policies were available for the government to use in 2009?

Fiscal policy

The circular flow of money shows how injections have a stimulating effect on the economy while leakages tend to depress economic activity. Fiscal policies such as public expenditure and tax cuts both help to stimulate the economy. Raising taxes and expenditure cuts can be used to stop the economy from growing unsustainably fast.

Keynes

These policies are associated with the work of J.M. Keynes (1883-1946). Much of his time was spent teaching at Cambridge University but he also worked for the UK government almost all of his adult life. In the Great Depression of the 1930s he saw that public spending could be increased through expansionary fiscal policies. This would help the economy to climb out of depression faster. If the economy was growing unsustainably fast and inflation was accelerating, fiscal policies could be reversed with tax increases and expenditure cuts.

> **Unsustainable economic growth** occurs when rising aggregate demand leads to accelerating inflation.
>
> **Fiscal policy** refers to the use of taxation to provide public services; it is also used to stimulate the economy or to slow the rate of economic growth. Fiscal policies must be used with care, and allowance must be made for possible time lags, if they are to be effective.

Keynes' policies were not implemented in the 1930s but post-war governments did use fiscal policy to encourage growth. However, in the 1980s they were blamed for accelerating inflation. Also, high taxes designed to provide better public services became less popular with voters.

UK direct and indirect taxes

Income tax

Income taxes are deducted at source by employers. Self-employed people submit a tax return. Council tax is based on the value of the property and is paid to the local council. Corporation tax is a tax on business profits. Inheritance tax is paid by people who inherit money above £320,000. Capital gains tax is paid when investments are sold; it reflects the amount by which the value of the capital item has grown since it was bought. All of these are direct taxes.

VAT

Indirect taxes are usually sales taxes – you pay nothing until you buy something. They include VAT, excise duties and duties on imports. VAT is a 20% sales tax on most products, except food eaten at home, children's clothing, public transport and housing. It is a percentage of the value added at each stage in production. Excise duties tax specific products, e.g. petrol, alcohol and tobacco (demerit goods). Import duties tax imports entering the country. (These have been considerably reduced over several decades through trade agreements.)

Direct taxes other than council tax help to redistribute income and reduce inequality because richer people and businesses pay more. Indirect taxes and council tax bear more heavily on people with lower incomes than on those with higher incomes. They seldom reduce inequality.

The role of the Bank of England and the Monetary Policy Committee (MPC)

Interest rates

Until 1997, governments could instruct the Bank of England to change the base rate. A lower base rate would stimulate economic activity and vice versa. There was a great temptation to cut interest rates a year or two ahead of elections, to be sure that prosperity would encourage voters to support the incumbent government. If this raised the rate of inflation, it would do so after the election and the government was safe for five more years. This system tended to cause instability.

It was clear that an independent central bank would produce better economic results. The Governor of the Bank of England, Mark Carney, chairs the MPC. Four more members are Bank of England employees; four others are respected independent economists. They spend time studying the data, then meet for two days a month to discuss the best course of action. Inflation has not been a serious problem at any time since the MPC was set up.

The Fed and the ECB

Many other countries have independent central banks; examples include the Federal Reserve Bank (the Fed) in the USA and the European Central Bank, (the ECB, in Frankfurt). Independence makes it much more likely that monetary policy decisions will maintain stability in the economy.

The MPC is charged with adjusting interest rates to maintain stability. Its target is a CPI inflation rate of 2%. Each month it sets the base rate of interest (0.5% from March 2009 to July 2016). This influences all other rates of interest in the economy. Higher interest rates will reduce borrowing and spending and vice versa. Besides inflation, the MPC studies employment and unemployment rates and the exchange rate, all of which can be important indicators that help to guide their decisions. In particular, higher interest rates may attract foreign investment and therefore increase demand for the pound, pushing up the exchange rate. This in turn makes imports cheaper.

Target 2%

The 2% target for inflation was chosen for very good reasons. Inflation above 2% is liable to accelerate and once inflation takes hold, it can be hard to reverse. A modest level of inflation helps the economy to adapt to change. Inflation between 0% and 2% has drawbacks. If some prices are falling, buyers may wait for them to fall further before making purchases. This has a depressing effect on the economy.

Show your understanding

The low interest rates prevailing since 2009 reflect the need for stimulus since the financial crisis and the subsequent recession. This is unprecedented – never before have interest rates been so low or low for so long. In July 2016, base rate was cut from 0.5% to 0.25%. The MPC observed slowing growth and a need for stimulus.

Low interest rates

1. Draw a flow chart that shows the sequence of events after a cut in interest rates.

2. Show the effects upon both businesses and consumers.

3. Discuss the reasons why the MPC thought the change was needed.

Find out

Inflation was very low in 2016. What has happened since? If it changed, what caused the change? How were economic policies adjusted as a result of the change? What effect did they have?

What if expansionary policies aren't working?

QE

After the financial crisis in 2009-10, most economies found that conventional expansionary policies were not working. Economic growth was either slow or negative. The central banks came up with **quantitative easing**, also called asset purchases. The assets concerned were mainly **government bonds**, many of which are held by banks. The central banks bought bonds, paying for them with cash. The hope was that the banks would use this money to lend to businesses for investment. It was a way of stimulating the economy when interest rates were already so low that any further reduction would be unlikely to help.

> **Bonds** may be issued by the central bank, to raise funds for the government, or by big businesses, to fund investment and expansion. Bonds are bought by banks, pension funds and insurance companies (and sometimes by individuals or businesses) because they are safe investments.
>
> **Quantitative easing (QE)** is an unconventional monetary policy aiming to stimulate bank lending by paying the banks in cash for bonds, which are less liquid.

The US Fed began QE in late 2008, immediately after the financial crisis. The Bank of England followed suit from 2009-12. Although the response was slow, the US was the first economy to begin recovery, around 2010. The UK began to grow steadily late in 2012 (see Figure 1). The ECB (European Central Bank) did not adopt QE until 2015 and started it cautiously.

Figure 1: GDP growth in the UK

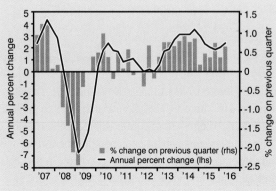

Source: ONS

Aggregate demand and the economy as a whole

Expansion

Both fiscal and monetary policies can have an expansionary effect. AD will grow and many businesses will increase output and take on more labour. If they also start to invest, that too will be a further injection into the circular flow of money. The UK saw this kind of recovery in the period 2012-2015.

Boom conditions include strong economic growth, high levels of investment and optimism. Unemployment will be low and this means that businesses may find it hard to recruit the people they want. They compete for people with scarce skills, offering higher pay. Inflation starts to accelerate because the economy is nearing full employment or full capacity output. Go back to Figure 1, Chapter 12 page 64, which illustrates this situation. The closer aggregate demand gets to full capacity output, the greater the inflationary pressures.

Contraction

When the economy overheats and there are skill shortages and inflation threatens, contractionary policies will be appropriate.

Watch out!
When drawing a diagram, make sure you place the AD curve so that it represents the actual situation. In boom conditions you must show AD crossing AS close to the point where inflation is rising. If you are showing the effect of increasing AD where there is spare capacity, the curve should be further to the left.

Show your understanding
1. Explain three ways in which fiscal and monetary policy might be used to reduce inflation. How might time lags affect the actual outcome?

2. Draw an AS/AD diagram that illustrates the effect of contractionary policies on prices.

Time lags

Most policy changes involve **time lags** – businesses and people take time to adjust. A change in interest rates or increased government spending may take a year or two to reach its full effect. Unemployment is usually lagged to the level of output by around 18 months. However a change in tax rates may affect AD much more quickly; it affects disposable income immediately. Once AD is growing and expectations are rosier, businesses will want to invest and produce more, so the economy enters a virtuous circle for as long as it has enough resources to expand without generating higher inflation.

A change in interest rates or increased government spending may take a year or two to reach its full effect.

Investment, job creation and economic growth

All of these are associated with the economic cycle: they will be observed first in the recovery process and then in a boom. Expansionary fiscal and monetary policies make it worthwhile for businesses to invest and recruit; consumer demand will grow. In time there may be a risk of overheating, bottlenecks (skill shortages) and inflation. But in recent years, other factors have made this less likely.

New technologies

- Supply-side policies (Chapter 14) may help to increase the supply of scarce skills by improving education and training.

- New technologies may make production more efficient.

- Cheap imports may help to keep inflation down.

- Employers may be able to recruit skilled people from overseas.

These influences were at work during the long period known as 'The Great Stability', from the mid 1990s to 2006. AS increased sufficiently for AD to grow steadily. Current low interest rates are designed to help businesses to get cheap loans and invest. Although this is potentially helpful, firms considering investment will want to know that there will be sufficient demand for their products.

Controlling inflation and unemployment

Fiscal and monetary policies play their part in controlling inflation and unemployment. Expansionary policies help to reduce demand deficiency unemployment. However, if the unemployment is structural, then expansionary policies will have little effect.

Structural unemployment

Structural unemployment is caused by shifting patterns of demand, for example caused by changing consumer preferences and competition from imports. It will last longer and affect more people if there is geographical and occupational immobility. Reducing this kind of unemployment requires supply-side policies (Chapter 14).

Contractionary policies normally help to control demand-pull inflation. However, cost-push inflation may be very persistent, or be imported. Fiscal and monetary policies may help to reduce it but the time lags are very long and much output may be lost.

Cost-inflation

> **Example**
> During the Thatcher era, the 1980s, inflation was high partly because of rising oil prices. This made many products more expensive. Tight fiscal and monetary policies were implemented. By the time inflation was damped down, 3 million people were unemployed. Inflation had had a destabilising effect, but the price paid to reduce it was felt by many to be excessive and perhaps, unnecessary. Combining fiscal, monetary and supply-side policies, carefully implemented, may achieve more at less cost.

Strengths, weaknesses and policy conflicts

- In the recession 2008-12, it was difficult for governments to adopt expansionary fiscal policies because they had spent vast sums bailing out banks. This produced deep anxiety about the size of the public sector deficit. After 2010, austerity policies such as public expenditure cuts did nothing to encourage economic growth and led to many redundancies.

- When structural reforms are needed – such as better skills training – expansionary policies are likely to lead to higher inflation rather than stronger growth.

- A very low base rate gives little scope for reducing it further, it may be of little use in encouraging growth.

- It can be difficult to achieve low inflation rates together with low unemployment – there is often a trade-off. However, the period 2000-2006 came very close to this.

Used carefully and in conjunction with supply-side policies, demand-side policies can be very effective. But finding the best package of policies may be demanding for politicians whose thinking lacks flexibility.

Exam style question (Paper 3)

Evidence A – The National Debt

A public sector deficit means that government spending exceeds its tax revenues, forcing it to borrow and so increasing the national debt. The UK Government owes more than £1.6 trillion to its creditors. That number is too big to comprehend. It is equivalent to £25,000 for each member of the population. In the financial crisis, the government bought bank shares to keep the banks in business, increasing public debt rapidly. Though Chancellor, George Osborne, prioritised reducing this debt and cut spending, the total kept increasing (though at a lower rate). His priority was abandoned in July, 2016.

Economists prefer to measure the government debt as a proportion of GDP rather than in money terms. On that basis, the debt is around 80% of GDP. This worries many people, but is modest compared to over 200% in 1945. Since 1945, governments have borrowed more than they have paid back, yet the debt to GDP ratio has fallen. There are two reasons for this. If GDP grows, the debt will fall as a share of GDP. When long run GDP growth was averaging more than 2% per year, that helped. Inflation reduces the real value of past borrowing and pushes up the money value of GDP by more than the real change.

There is a downside to public borrowing and debt if it pushes up interest rates and crowds out private sector activity. On this basis, borrowing during a boom would be particularly dangerous. However, austerity with low growth is a more painful and less effective route to debt reduction than GDP growth and mild inflation.

Evidence B – UK Quantitative Easing

The Bank of England buys assets, usually government bonds, with money created electronically. This increases liquidity in the financial system, so banks can lend more to businesses and individuals. This could stimulate aggregate demand. The Bank created £375bn of new money via QE between 2009 and 2012. MPC member Martin Wheale estimated that this added about 3% to GDP.

Business groups complained that buying government bonds rather than bonds from firms did little for the real economy. There was little improvement in access to loans for small and medium sized companies struggling to stay afloat. The Bank itself said that wealthy families were the biggest beneficiaries of QE, thanks to the resulting rise in share and bond values.

Adapted from BankofEngland.co.uk and *The Guardian*, 22 June 2015

Questions

a) Discuss the suggestion that the national debt is a burden to future generations. *(8 marks)*

b) Assess the merits of measuring national debt as a percentage of GDP. *(10 marks)*

c) Assess reasons why quantitative easing might not improve access to loans for small firms. *(12 marks)*

d) Evaluate the relative merits of quantitative easing and a fiscal stimulus at a time of recession. *(20 marks)*

Terms to revise: supply-side policies, productivity, efficiency, lean production, the CMA and competition law, infrastructure.

Skill shortages and apprenticeships

Britain has a chronic skills shortage. Many UK businesses recruit from abroad. There is a global shortage of engineering skills. Britain also has unemployed young people. Figure 1 shows that unemployment for 16-24 year-olds reached 20% in 2010. By 2016, that had fallen but still, one in seven young people were unemployed.

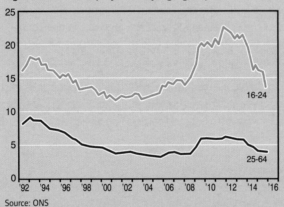

Figure 1: UK unemployment by age group, %

Source: ONS

High unemployment means wasted resources. Skill shortages combined with youth unemployment indicate a skills mismatch. In late 2014, Crossrail, the builders of London's newest railway line, appealed for more women to train as engineers to avert the skills shortage.

During the government expenditure cuts in the period 2010-15, investment in education and skills, research and science were all squeezed. George Osborne, the then Chancellor, really wanted to shrink the public sector. By 2015 he thought that neglecting skills training might be unwise. He planned an apprenticeship levy, a tax on all employers with a pay bill above £3m. This was expected to bring in £3bn a year, which could be used to help fund new and enhanced training schemes.

Discussion points

How will better training provision affect the economy?

Many businesses dislike the idea of the apprenticeship levy. Why might this be?

Why have market forces failed to produce enough people with the skills that are in demand?

Market-based and interventionist policies

Demand–side policies are by their nature macro-economic policies – they affect the whole economy. Many **supply-side policies** are micro-economic in nature – they affect particular elements of the economy.

In a free market system, businesses decide for themselves what they should do about training people in the skills they require. Market forces should ensure that the training provided is exactly what the employers require. Traditionally businesses have been free to make their own training arrangements. However, many businesses have chosen a minimalist approach and the result has been frequent skill shortages. This may happen when shareholders are pressing for short-term profit rather than long term growth. Training can be costly and the benefits are long-term. This is market failure – training is under-produced.

Market-based policies aim to remove barriers that prevent free markets from working efficiently. Where there is limited competition, output is lower and prices are higher than they need to be. Competition policy can increase efficiency by forcing businesses to compete. Privatisation may also lead to increased efficiency, provided there is genuine competition. This policy worked with BT – it became more efficient and prices fell. Some deregulation allows positive developments that could not occur in a heavily regulated market.

Insufficient training

Some market-based policies spring from a belief in 'smaller government', which implies lower taxes and less government expenditure, i.e. fewer public services. The idea is that businesses will invest more and create jobs while individuals will have more of an incentive to work. This is controversial: it might increase economic growth but it would probably also increase inequality.

Intervention-ist policies

Governments may use **interventionist policies** to address problems related to market failure. The apprenticeship levy is an example. It is designed to make the labour market work better but it is not a free-market policy because it gives bigger businesses no choice.

> **Supply-side policies** include all measures that can increase the total productive capacity of the economy. They work to increase output using existing resources.
>
> **Market-based policies** work on the principle that free markets can deliver both productive and allocative efficiency. They are intended to remove impediments to economic growth.
>
> **Interventionist policies** influence and control market forces in order to correct for market failure and imperfect competition.

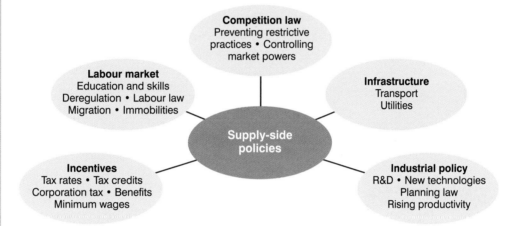

Labour market issues

High youth unemployment and skill shortages indicate a mismatch within the labour market. Skill shortages make it hard to increase long-run aggregate supply, the key to economic growth. They are a significant cause of the supply constraints that occur when aggregate demand is growing close to full capacity output. Intervention may be necessary to avoid this. Take another look at Figure 1: high youth unemployment in the UK is a significant waste of resources.

Efficiency

Supply-side policies that improve education and training should improve the efficiency of the labour market and provide the necessary resources for business expansion and rising AS. The apprenticeship levy is an interventionist policy that requires employers to pay for vocational training. An alternative to improving education and training is to ensure that migration law allows employers to recruit skilled people from abroad.

> **Find out**
> Are apprenticeships creating more employment opportunities? Has the apprenticeship levy actually come into force? In 2016, employers, worried about the effect of Brexit, called for it to be delayed. If it is, how might this affect the economy?

Reducing immobilities

Some unemployment is due to redundancies from declining industries (or even just changing consumer preferences). People with a range of skills can find work relatively quickly but those who really only know how to work in one specific occupation have more difficulty. Interventionist schemes can reduce immobilities, helping unemployed people to acquire new skills and also travel further to work. This reduces supply constraints, enabling structurally unemployed people to find jobs and add to aggregate supply.

Labour market law

Government intervention has created labour law and related regulations that lay down requirements for employers. Many of these prevent dangerous working practices and set standards for working conditions. Employment protection legislation sets conditions for making employees redundant and employers need to understand these. Some regulations annoy some employers but many are greatly valued by their employees.

It is important not to make it impossible for employers to make employees redundant. This makes employers very cautious about recruiting and leads to fewer jobs being created.

Employment protection

Example
UK law insists that people made redundant have some rights but it does not require employers to keep them on if there is nothing they can do. France has much tighter employment protection and as a consequence, unemployment rates are higher. (They have been around 10-12% for many years.) Germany also had more labour regulation than the UK but set about reforming its labour law shortly before the financial crisis. This has reduced unemployment levels, though not to UK rates. Employment protection is a big issue for many governments. Reforming employment law is often advocated by bodies such as the IMF. It may be referred to as structural reform. Only Canada and the USA have lighter employment regulation than the UK.

Flexibility

The UK labour market is more flexible than most. This makes it easier for businesses to respond to changing patterns of demand. These can be caused by changes in consumer preferences, or cheap imports or new products and new technologies. A flexible labour market helps businesses to take advantage of new markets and adapt to change. That flexibility in itself helps to ensure that resources are used in the most efficient way, and new jobs are created.

The downside to the UK's labour market flexibility and lighter labour laws is that many of the extra jobs created have part-time or zero hours contracts. During the period 2012-2015 around one million employees wanted a full time job but accepted part-time work because there was no alternative. Full-time jobs for them could potentially add to AS.

Incentives

People vary greatly in their opinions about incentives. Free-market enthusiasts say that low benefits are an incentive to work. Low tax rates give highly paid people an incentive to work harder. Low corporation taxes (business taxes on profits) provide an incentive to invest. For interventionists, low benefits simply create unacceptable poverty.

Which incentives work?

Research has found no evidence that business managers and employers work harder if taxes are cut. Low corporation taxes may help to provide funds for investment but they may also lead simply to higher dividends for shareholders.

What is very clear is that low pay can be a significant disincentive to work. This is especially likely where unemployment benefits amount to more than the wages for available jobs, less the cost of working (travel costs etc). This is called the **poverty trap**. To get more unemployed people back into the

People vary greatly in their opinions about incentives.

Incentives to reduce unemployment

labour market, the **working families tax credit** system was introduced in 2009. It is an interventionist policy to ensure that people in work are always better off working than relying on benefits. It created an incentive that helped to reduce unemployment once the economy began to recover.

> The **poverty trap** becomes a problem when disposable income is lower than the benefit rate.
>
> **Tax credits**, as the **working families tax credit** is generally known now, create an incentive to work by ensuring that everyone is better off in work.

Higher minimum wage rates can give employers an incentive to provide more training so as to ensure that employee productivity rises. Higher labour productivity means that output increases without the need for an increase in the supply of labour.

Minimum wages

Show your understanding

Unfortunately, tax credits have made it easier for employers to get away with paying very low wages. So the cost of tax credits has risen, increasing government spending. To get around this the Chancellor introduced a big increase in the minimum wage in his 2016 Budget. By 2020, this will cut the cost of tax credits but could possibly reduce the number of jobs available. Employers may be happy to employ some people on very low wages but not if they cost more than that. There may be an incentive to make more people redundant. In the past this was never a problem – the introduction of minimum wages did not lead to any obvious increase in unemployment. But a bigger increase in the minimum wage may have more effect on employment.

1. Explain how a higher minimum wage will affect:
   * tax credits
   * incentives to work
   * employment and unemployment
   * productivity and output.

In the summer of 2016, many trade associations wrote jointly to Greg Clark, the business secretary, asking that he *'exercise caution'* on the national living wage in the light of *'economic uncertainties the country faces'* after the Brexit vote.

2. Outline ways of ensuring that incentives to work can be maintained.

Competition law

The CMA exists to penalise businesses that engage in restrictive practices that distort prices. It ensures that no one business has excessive power in its market. Market power gives businesses a chance to reduce quantities supplied and charge higher prices. For the market as a whole this reduces efficiency. Chapter 7 provides many examples of anti-competitive practices, such as price fixing and tacit collusion, that raise prices and distort the allocation of resources. Keeping markets working well requires interventionist policies that can enforce the rules.

Lean production

Competition forces businesses to keep their production costs to a minimum and prices as low as possible. Competitive businesses may implement lean production strategies. Minimising waste is a good way to optimise resource allocation.

Infrastructure

Roads and bridges are almost always provided by government, local or national. Ports, airports, the railways, telecommunications, water and energy are mostly provided by the private sector but very carefully controlled by regulators. Many of these are natural monopolies; there are very large economies of scale and in some cases a risk of expensive duplication. Water supplies, drainage and the railways are the most obvious.

That said, governments are likely to be heavily involved in any major infrastructure development. The UK is often said to have weak infrastructure, compared to other similar economies. Infrastructure improvements would remove awkward supply constraints. Government intervention can ease congestion on roads and railways.

Less congestion, fewer bottlenecks

Example
When it became clear that London's airport capacity needed to be increased, politicians proposed a range of options and there was a long debate about the best course of action. You might conclude that decisive intervention to decide where the additional runway will be would help.

Infrastructure projects need money. This means that they will be competing with a whole range of public services, all of which require additional funding. Austerity policies may cause politicians to disagree about the priorities. From the point of view of the economy this is unfortunate because investment in infrastructure will often pay for itself in the long run by cutting the costs of congestion and speeding up transport and communication.

Private finance initiatives (PFI) have been used to fund infrastructure (see Chapter 11, pages 58-9). This funding comes from the private sector but the costs of this approach may be higher than the cost of government borrowing, especially when base rate is low. This may turn out to be an example of government failure rather than market failure.

Industrial policy

When free-market policies have been fashionable, politicians have tended to conclude that having an industrial policy is unnecessary and unhelpful. However, when Theresa May became prime minister in 2016 she included amongst her objectives creating an industrial policy that would seek to benefit all parts of the UK – not just the prosperous south east. This might highlight some particular needs that may have been neglected in the past.

Find out
whether an industrial policy has come to fruition, and what the priorities now are. What supply-side policies have been included?

An industrial policy might place emphasis on developing the following:

● **New technologies** that can enable businesses to extend their product range (product innovation) or cut costs of production (through process innovation). This can help the public sector as well as the private sector.

● **Research and development** similarly create new ways of producing as well as new products.

Addressing supply constraints

Example
Medical research has shown that some people who might in the past have needed hospital treatment can be given exercises to do at home, or medicines that are now manufactured relatively cheaply. This can save the NHS considerable sums of money.

● **Process innovation** often increases productivity. Government spending on research can become an external economy of scale for many businesses. This will help to make UK products more competitive on international markets. Healthy export levels are important in fostering economic growth.

● Adjusting **planning laws** could free up more space for development. For many years, land for building homes, factories and office buildings has been very scarce because of planning rules. This is a major supply constraint.

Strengths and weakness of supply-side policies

Supply-side policies are potentially very powerful. Many satisfy a range of different viewpoints and expectations. Better education and skills, more R&D and encouraging the use of new technologies would be supported by many politicians, businesses and individuals. All supply-side policies are intended to enhance economic growth without causing accelerating inflation. Creating incentives for low-paid people to work should ultimately reduce benefits, improve incomes and lead to training opportunities as well as increasing AS.

Competition policies can deal with businesses that have a vested interest in restricting output. Deregulation may be popular but it may also worsen working conditions for many.

Long time lags

Almost all supply-side policies take a long time to develop successfully. They may require funding immediately in the hope of a very worthwhile outcome in the future. Improved education can take decades to bear fruit. Governments, with their five-year time horizons, may be hesitant about setting up policies that will not start to help the economy until long after their term of office is up.

Interventionist policies can lead to government failure if they are not implemented appropriately. They may eliminate one distortion but create another. National Insurance Charges (NICs) help to fund the NHS and pensions but they also act as a tax on employment. Businesses that want to take on more labour will have to pay the employer's NIC as well as the wages and salaries of their new employees. This may limit job creation.

Policy conflicts and trade-offs

Export prospects

After the 2016 referendum, the exchange rate fell sharply. Uncertainty and reduced levels of foreign direct investment (FDI) seemed very likely to keep the exchange rate low for some time to come. This could make UK exports more competitive. If, also, supply-side policies can be used to enhance competitiveness in the long run, the UK might be able to avoid the recession that most economists expect to develop. It will be important to be able to increase aggregate supply in order to take advantage of export opportunities.

Many supporters of Brexit also support smaller government, austerity policies and free market solutions. There may be trade-offs between a preference for free-market policies and the political objective of reducing the imbalance in incomes and wealth between south-east England and London, and the rest of the UK. Spending on infrastructure can increase government expenditure.

> **Example**
> Transport facilities in the northeast of England, which has the lowest average income of all the English regions, have been neglected. This makes reducing unemployment harder and makes it a less attractive place for businesses to invest. There is a need for spending on infrastructure to get the region growing again. This may not be consistent with restricting public expenditure.

Maintaining a flexible labour force means accepting redundancies when patterns of demand change. Popular policies such as deregulation may have very detrimental effects on individuals' quality of life and create long-term environmental problems that affect future generations.

> **Show your understanding**
> 1. Identify one other trade-off that may affect aggregate supply.
> 2. Draw an AS/AD diagram that illustrates the impact of increased government expenditure. Use it to analyse the likely outcome, in today's situation.
> 3. Explain why this might be a viable policy.

Chapter 15

The impact of macroeconomic policies

The Labour government approach, 1997

In the May election, after 18 years in opposition, Labour won a landslide majority of 179 seats. It was its largest Parliamentary majority since 1935. To be absolutely sure of winning, Gordon Brown, the Chancellor, had promised that there would be no tax increases for two years.

For the Chancellor, key concerns were the unemployment rate, which was still rather high, and inflation, which was low but not as low as economists would recommend. The manifesto had promised no tax increases for two years, so big increases in public spending were out of the question.

The priorities were:

● Economic stability to promote investment.

● A tough inflation target of 2.5%.

● Improvements in education and training so that the workforce would more closely match the requirements of employers.

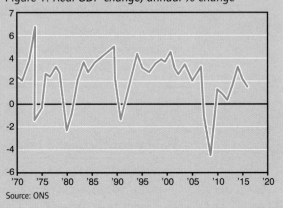

Figure 1: Real GDP change, annual % change

Source: ONS

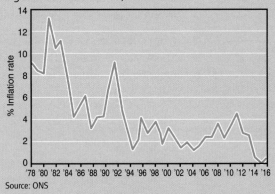

Figure 2: Inflation rates, 1980-2016

Source: ONS

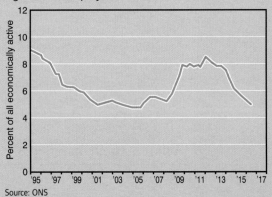

Figure 3: Unemployment (LFS)

Source: ONS

Discussion points

How would you describe the state of the UK economy in 1997?

Identify fiscal, monetary and supply-side policies that would be relevant in the 1997 situation, given the Chancellor's objectives.

Using the data in Figures 1, 2 and 3, comment on the actual outcome of the government's policies.

Policy packages

Combining policies

Most economic strategies require a combination of policies. This will depend partly on the time that each policy takes to produce results (i.e. possible time lags) and partly on the issues of the moment. The economy was fairly stable in 1997. The Chancellor took advantage of this to introduce a new way of determining monetary policies. He made the Bank of England independent and responsible for the inflation target. It was hoped that this would make accelerating inflation less likely in the future. Politicians could no longer introduce monetary policies that promised rapid growth just before an election. (See page 71 for more on this.)

Taxes could not be increased so spending on public services had to be controlled. The Chancellor's package focused on monetary policy reform and supply-side policies.

Expansionary policies	Contractionary policies	Supply-side policies
Tax cuts	Tax increases	Incentives to work
More government spending	Government spending cuts	Education and training
Lower interest rates	Higher interest rates	Infrastructure
		Competition

Think!

At times, we find that there is a trade-off between inflation and unemployment. Explain why this may happen. Under what circumstances might it be possible to have low inflation and low unemployment? To what extent does productivity affect the macro-economy?

A recession policy package

2010

Cut to 2010

The financial crisis 2008-9 created very stressful situations for policy-makers. In 2010 there was an election, bringing to power a coalition government led by the Conservatives with a strong input from the Liberal Democrats. They faced a startlingly different scenario from 1997. In particular there was a big public sector deficit. The Labour government had spent some money on public services, especially the NHS, but the main cause was the amount of money needed to bail out the banks in 2009. The economy was still in recession; economic growth had inched up above zero but was still very slow.

Think!

Devise a policy package appropriate for the situation in 2010. Keep in mind that the Bank of England's base rate was static at 0.5%, i.e. very low. What options did the government have? Don't forget to allow for time lags.

What actually happened

Chancellor George Osborne's primary objective was to cut the deficit every year and get it down to zero by 2020. This required austerity budgets. The way he put it to the public emphasised the future burden for our children and grandchildren of paying back the debt. Both major political parties supported austerity.

Austerity

The Chancellor was confident that austerity would not impede economic growth. He made substantial government expenditure cuts; nearly 1 million people in the public sector were made redundant. He also managed to meet another of his objectives. He badly wanted 'smaller government'. This is a significant objective for all free market thinkers; it implies lower taxes and limited public services.

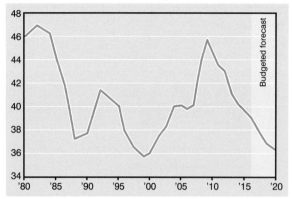

Figure 4: Current public spending as % of GDP*

Source: OBR   *Excludes investment

Deficit reduction

Figure 4 shows that the Osborne objectives were, to a considerable extent, met. In the aftermath of the financial crisis, public spending rose above 45% of GDP. By the time of Osborne's departure from government, it had fallen to 39%. The government role in the economy is already substantially smaller. It may or may not reach the 35% target in 2020. Theresa May has suggested that there is a need for spending on currently neglected areas and communities that have not benefited greatly from recent economic growth.

Was there an alternative?

Many economists would argue that austerity caused a much longer recession than necessary. Up to 2013, the economy remained very sluggish and briefly fell back into negative growth territory, just for one quarter. Then suddenly in 2014, growth registered 3.2%. The UK became the fastest growing economy in the EU. (See Figure 1, page 82.)

Early return to growth

An alternative policy would have involved avoiding government spending cuts and shrinking public services. There would have been an earlier return to growth, with higher tax revenues and less spending on benefits for unemployed people. This would have helped to reduce the public sector deficit.

If money had been channeled towards building infrastructure, economic growth would have been even stronger. Unemployment would have fallen faster.

> **Show your understanding**
> To what extent did your policy package for 2010 differ from Mr Osborne's? Comment on any differences and consider the pros and cons of both packages. Explain each element of the package and its likely effect. (If your policy package was similar to Mr Osborne's compare this with the alternative detailed above.) Draw AS/AD diagrams that indicate the outcomes of both approaches.

Other aspects of economic policy

So far the focus of attention has been upon conventional fiscal, monetary and supply-side policies and their effect on economic growth. There are other policies and perspectives. You need to understand these in order to see the big picture more clearly.

Automatic stabilisers can work to reduce the impact of the economic cycle without any change in policy. As unemployment rises, government expenditure rises to cover the cost of benefits. Tax payments fall because incomes are falling. This provides an instant increase in injections and decrease in leakages that will tend to stimulate the economy, or at least reduce the impact of recession. The reverse happens as the economy recovers and should dampen the effect of a developing boom.

> **Automatic stabilisers** reduce the fluctuations of the economic cycle without requiring a change in fiscal policy. They reduce aggregate demand in a boom and increase it during a recession.

In recent years we have learnt much about how to achieve economic stability. Fiscal, monetary and supply-side policies all have their uses. The problems associated with the financial crisis may be largely eliminated by tighter banking regulation (Chapter 18). The package of policies that is chosen by the government will depend partly on political preferences. It will also be affected by many other influences.

New technologies

- **Changing technologies** have a big impact on economies. They increase productivity and often contribute to economic growth but they also create structural unemployment. Governments that try to reduce unemployment by using expansionary policies may discover that their unemployment is not cyclical but structural. Only supply-side policies can permanently reduce structural unemployment.

- **Reactions to inequality** may rule out some policies. If growing numbers of people are experiencing reduced incomes, some of these will be facing poverty that is not acceptable in a civilised society. Other policies may be required to deal with homelessness, struggling schools and hospitals. Government expenditure cuts are apt to lead to pockets of very severe deprivation that affect children in a way that is detrimental to the long-term future of the economy.

- **Globalisation** has lifted billions of people out of poverty. However, increasing specialisation always creates losers as well as gainers. If the needs of the losers are not addressed, their opposition to policies that have long-run potential may drag down economic growth for all, including themselves.

Vested interests

- **Vested interests** can work against good policy making. Businesses lobby governments to adjust policy to suit their own interests rather than those of the whole population. Monopolies use their power to stand in the way of competition. Monopolies include businesses, employers' associations and trade unions. Pressure groups may lobby to get policies that are not actually in the interests of all. Promoting competition helps to reduce the influence of vested interests.

- **Climate change** introduces very serious challenges for some governments and may affect the economy considerably. Where current trends are very economically destructive there will be major conflicts of interest. Early action would reduce the impact of climate change.

> **Think!**
> Achieving stability in the modern world can pose tough problems that many people would like to ignore. As beginner economists, you should feel very good about the fact that you are learning to understand how the world really works. Ignorance is a major barrier to competent economic policy making. But economies are very complex. List six problems that you consider to be significant. Ask yourself, can these objectives all be met at once? To what extent might they conflict?

Comparing alternative approaches

In the past some clearly contrasting theories have influenced policy making. It is useful to look at how these have affected policy over the years since World War II. You have already come across J.M. Keynes, (page 70) who gave his name to the Keynesian approach, which dominated policy-making from the 1940s to the '70s. With the election of Mrs Thatcher in 1979 came the monetarist approach, based on the work of Milton Friedman and other free market economists.

Since the 1990s, policies have often drawn on both approaches. Current policies are likely to be dominated by uncertainty and some considerable difficulties as yet unknown, because we know very little about the conditions that will accompany the process of leaving the EU.

Keynesian policies 1945-1979 → Monetarist policies 1979-1997 → New labour approach 1997-2010 → Austerity 2010-2016 → Policy dominated by changes associated with leaving the EU

Keynes showed that unemployment could persist for a long time before market forces eventually generated increasing levels of demand.

Keynesian policy – intervention

Persistent unemployment

The basic insight that Keynes gave us is that the economy may settle at an equilibrium level of output that leaves many people unemployed. He showed that this unemployment could persist for a long time before market forces eventually generated increasing levels of demand. He wrote his major works during the Great Depression of the 1930s. He advocated increasing public spending, financed by borrowing, that would stimulate economic activity and create jobs. His views underpin all of the approaches that feed into expansionary policies. Keynesian policies were often referred to as interventionist.

Keynes understood that AD might increase to the point where inflation becomes a problem. His views were based on the assumption that policies would be adjusted in the event of a boom. In practice, politicians tended to let expansionary policies last for too long, creating inflation and instability.

Monetarist policies – the free market

Milton Friedman spent most of his working life at the University of Chicago. He observed that Keynesian policies might lead to rapid expansion and accelerating inflation. His theories showed that stability would best be achieved by leaving the economy to evolve through free market forces alone. He held that very high rates of interest would be the best weapon against inflation. He believed that simply announcing an increase in interest rates would dampen expectations immediately and lead to a swift adjustment of the economy and the inflation rate.

Public expenditure cuts

When Mrs Thatcher arrived at Number 10, the base rate was already 12%; the previous government understood that inflation was a real problem. The base rate was raised to 17% and there were also big public expenditure cuts. The inflation rate fell fast, but unemployment rose from just over 1 million to more than 3 million in 1984. The hardship for many individuals was very serious indeed. Not until the late 1990s did employment levels really recover.

Although monetarism had a significant downside in terms of its impact on employment, elements of it are still visible. George Osborne's preference for smaller government and Republican policies in the USA still reflect monetarist arguments. In practice both the Keynesian and the monetarist arguments offer insights that can help in the process of policy formulation.

Austerity policies

Austerity leads to slower economic growth, recession and lower incomes. Inevitably, tax revenue falls. This may make the deficit larger. In practice it appears that Mr Osborne understood this because his expenditure cuts were never quite so big as his original proposals. Nevertheless the austerity policies did prolong the recession.

Environmental problems tend to go hand in hand with economic growth. Slower growth can allow more time to get environmentally friendly policies working.

Greece

> **Find out**
> Austerity policies were applied to Greece when it became clear that it needed huge loans after the financial crisis. Tax revenue fell. A basic problem was that Greece found it very hard to compete with the rest of the eurozone. Think carefully about the effect of continuing austerity on the Greek economy. N.B. in 2016, the IMF urged Germany to provide more cash to reduce the impact of austerity measures on the Greek economy.

Evaluating effectiveness

Evaluation has a tendency to reflect political preferences. However, the good economist looks closely at the evidence and works out the implications without reference to personal opinions.

Policy objectives

● Policy objectives must be identified. Outcomes can be evaluated according to whether the objectives have been met.

● Next, the economist looks at the full range of consequences that the policy has created. There will be an impact on the economy as a whole and on specific groups of people within the population. Unintended consequences may have created costs even if the original policy objective has been met.

Allowances have to be made for unexpected shocks and events. These may derail a policy that when formulated, looked sensible. Policy conflicts must be considered too. It would not be unusual for a government to pursue two conflicting objectives without exploring the likelihood of a trade-off.

Criteria for success have to relate to specific objectives. Did austerity policies reduce the deficit? The answer for the UK is yes. They reduced it by nearly half, but it remained rather high. Most Greeks would suggest that the answer is no.

> **Show your understanding**
> 1. Did counter-inflation policies reduce the rate of inflation? How?
> 2. Did low interest rates lead to increased investment? Explain how the policies were supposed to work and how they actually worked, or not. If not, explain why.
> 3. Identify trade-offs that governments may face when creating economic policy packages.

The impact of tax credits

Tax credits were introduced in 2009 by the Labour government. They were designed to eliminate the poverty trap and create an incentive to work. In 2015, the Chancellor threatened to abolish them but settled for a reduction in the costs. Most people think every adult should be in work. An incentive to work makes people less likely to fall back into the poverty trap (where benefits are higher than the wages on offer where there are job vacancies). This is a supply-side policy because it has potential to increase output. It could also be seen as a fiscal policy because it reduces the cost of benefits.

Unemployment fell

As a result of tax credits, many unemployed people found work. Often it was poorly paid but the tax credits still made it worth working. Like most economic policies it took some time to work but by 2012, unemployment was falling.

An unintended consequence was that many people who found work received very low pay. Employers were pleased. Rates of pay for unskilled jobs actually fell. The bill for the tax credits got bigger and bigger. This did not chime with austerity. In his 2016 Budget statement Mr Osborne raised the minimum wage, planned to be £9 per hour in 2020. This should reduce the need for tax credits but may or may not reduce the availability of jobs for unskilled people.

Watch this space

Confidence and Brexit

Leaving the EU is widely expected to cause a recession and higher unemployment. Loss of confidence in the economic future, and uncertainty as to how trading relationships will change, seem likely to reduce investment in the UK, at least for a period of some years. There will probably be changes that amount to a shock to the economy. If the changes are very major, it may take decades to complete the economic adjustments. Individual policies are subject to time lags but a whole series of changes may require much longer. The expected recession could appear towards the end of 2017 or later.

Indeed these uncertainties may make it hard to evaluate all economic policies for a while. Examiners may award marks for explaining the economic consequences of particular policies in 'normal' circumstances. But don't forget to explain why Brexit may cause a different outcome from the normal one.

Show your understanding

1. Explain the likely consequences of a recession. (This is most likely to happen after the UK has actually left the EU.)

2. In the event of recession, policies will be put in place to minimise its impact. Explain what policies these might be and consider how effective they might be. What kinds of problems might reduce their effectiveness?

Leaving the EU

The decision to leave the European Union made in June 2016 will have consequences for the economy for years to come, but the immediate effect of a fall in the exchange rate has mixed impacts on business. Claire Burrows, founder of London-based footwear brand Air & Grace said *"Our shoes are designed in the UK but manufactured in Europe and I buy my finished shoes in Euros from Portugal. If the pound falls by 10% the cost of purchasing shoes rises by 10%. There are two choices – let the business absorb the cost resulting in a reduced margin or passing it on to the consumer via increased retail prices. I've chosen to do the former, but it's not a viable long term strategy."*

At the same time, York-based jewellers Nightingale imports diamonds from the United States and reported a 5-10% increase in the cost of imports. Richard Hatfield (Director), said *"From a purely commercial perspective one benefit to come out of the weakness of the pound is that we are now more competitive as a retailer in foreign markets."*

Essay question

Evaluate some likely consequences of leaving the EU with reference to the examples above.

Chapter 16
Risk and uncertainty

Terms to revise: this chapter relies on knowledge of macroeconomic policies, risk and the financing of business investment (covered in Theme 1).

Shocks

Shocks

In 1973 oil prices suddenly shot up, from about US$3 to $12 per barrel. As shocks go, this was dramatic. OPEC (the Organisation of Petroleum Exporting Countries) realised that by limiting the amount of oil they pumped, they could make a lot more money. People suddenly had to pay about three times as much for a tank of petrol. So what happened to their spending on other things? Most of the developed world sank into a prolonged recession. (Google 'oil prices 1970s' and look at Wikipedia's graph.) They tried it again in 1979.

Other big past shocks include the unification of Germany (1989), the global financial crisis of 2008-9 and the Fukushima disaster in Japan, caused by the earthquake and tsunami in 2011.

Discussion points

Think about how higher petrol prices affected individuals and businesses.

Why did this shock have such a big impact?

What would be the likely impact of oil price rises in the future?

Using your knowledge of economics, work out the economic consequences of the Fukushima disaster.

We are very aware of **uncertainty**. We know that nature can surprise us with earthquakes and nations with wars. But the timing of these things is very uncertain so they create shocks to the economy. **Shocks** are events that have a dramatic impact and are, for most people, unexpected.

The oil price shock of 1973 is worth looking at because it is simple. OPEC is a cartel. The members made their decisions in secret. It could not have been predicted by oil users. Uncertainty is like this – there is no way to calculate the probabiiity of its happening. Any unexpected change in the political system will create uncertainty about possible changes in the law or regulation. In any market, suppliers may change their strategies, creating uncertainty for competing businesses.

Risks

Risks are different from uncertainty. If you have recently learnt to drive, you will know that insurance premiums are far higher for young people than for their parents. The insurance companies have vast amounts of data on the probability of accidents occurring within different age groups. They just crunch the numbers and set the premium at the level needed to cover the likely cost of claims. Past data tells them the relative risk levels for different age groups.

> **Shocks** are unexpected or unpredictable events that have a major effect on the national economy. Some affect the global economy too.
>
> **Uncertainty** refers to any possible change that is not predictable. There is no way to calculate its likelihood (probability).
>
> **Risks** arise when changes are expected; the probability of their happening can be calculated with some degree of accuracy, using past data.

Shocks and their impact: leaving the EU

Leaving the EU will create very significant shockwaves as changes take place, despite the fact that we know they are coming. The outcome is unpredictable; there will probably be unintended consequences. Most individuals and organisations will find that they need to adjust to the new situation. While these adjustments are being made, there will be many knock-on effects. Uncertainty will hamper rational decision taking both for businesses and governments.

Tariffs and exports

- If UK exporters face higher tariffs in their customer countries, their customers there will have to pay more to buy their products. Unless demand is price inelastic, sales are likely to fall. Exporting businesses may have to make employees redundant in order to survive; some may keep on their employees but pay them less in real terms.

- Falling exports may cause the exchange rate to depreciate. After a period of adjustment, exports would be cheaper; this would help exporters, making them more competitive. However, import prices would rise. This reduces consumers' spending power. For example they will probably have to pay more for imported clothing.

- Much of the FDI that has come into the UK from businesses outside the EU occurred because it allowed the investors to produce within the EU and avoid the CET. Once the UK leaves the EU, they will not get this benefit, so they are rather less likely to invest in the UK in future. This will reduce the demand for pounds on the foreign exchange markets, leading to a lower exchange rate.

Confused?
Go back to Theme 3 and revise exchange rates and trading blocs. These topics are important in this theme.

Show your understanding
Identify three different businesses that are likely to be affected when the UK leaves the EU. Explain the adjustments that they may have to make and the likely consequences for their stakeholders. If everything is settled by the time you are reading this, say how your chosen examples were affected.

Other shocks

Reunification of Germany

German reunification in 1989 created a great deal of unemployment. The East German factories were very inefficient and could not compete with West German (or other) producers. So many East German manufacturing organisations closed down; those made redundant were either unemployed for some time or moved west. Only fairly recently has the East German economy made real progress in recovering.

Falling oil prices

The oil price fall in 2014-15 had a devastating effect on the producer economies, especially those that have relatively low incomes, e.g. Nigeria and Venezuela. This was caused by slower growth in China's demand for oil, and a big increase in oil and gas supplies from US and Canadian fracking operations, increased production from Iraq as its economy recovered from war and new discoveries elsewhere. At the same time commodity prices were falling. Zambia's revenue from copper exports and Brazil's revenue from exports of coffee and soybeans sank. An underlying cause was slower growth in China.

That other big shock, the 2008-9 financial crisis, is covered in detail in Chapter 19, page 104.

Show your understanding
Shocks are many and varied but you can use the economics you have already learnt to deduce what will happen. Where you can, use diagrams to support your conclusions. Use timelines to explain the immediate, middle and long term effects.

1. Explain how falling oil prices affected the UK economy in 2015-16.

2. Work out how rising oil prices might affect the UK economy in the future.

3. Explain the impact on the Nigerian economy of the oil price fall, 2014-15.

Time lags

Adjusting to change takes time. Changes in employment usually occur 12-18 months after the changes that made them necessary. Businesses may take a similar length of time to grasp the implications of change and take action. Policy-makers have to review their existing policies. They may be able to make plans based on past experience but that may lead to mistakes if the current situation is very different from the past. If changing regulation is not sufficient, public debate and delays in the parliamentary process may lengthen the adjustment process.

Shocks are apt to create changes that take time to unfold. After Fukushima, some manufacturers were without power for some time. Others were destroyed. The supply of some car components for vehicle manufacturers elsewhere in Japan (and in other economies) dried up. These customers of the stricken factories had to find new sources of supply. This was not easy for highly technical products designed for specific models.

Labour immobilities

Even when solutions have been identified and implemented, further adjustments will be needed. Immobilities in the labour market slow down the process of change. In general, resistance to change within businesses may cause them to limp along when radical action might be more appropriate.

Exchange rate risks and forward markets.

You can see that many shocks hit home through the impact of the shock on exchange rates. In fact, exchange rates can create smaller shocks all on their own. Exporters and importers need to deal in foreign exchange all the time.

> **Think!**
> Majestic imports wines from all over the world. Supposing it has just ordered a large consignment of wine from France. The day after the order is placed, the pound depreciates against the euro. What happens to the price that Majestic has to pay? What will happen if this happens several times over the course of one year? Draw a flow chart that shows the sequence of events.

Depreciation

Depreciation can benefit exporters, making them more competitive. Appreciation has the reverse effect. Importers benefit from appreciation, which makes their products cheaper and vice versa. Exchange rate changes affect profits, incomes and employment opportunities.

After the Fukushima disaster some customers had to find new sources of supply due to factories being destroyed.

Forward markets

Exchange rate volatility affects all exporters and importers. However, they can reduce the uncertainty by buying currency in the **forward markets**. An importer buying forward in the foreign exchange market can buy the currency they will need to pay for the imports later at a set price, now. This removes the uncertainty. Of course, if the exchange rate stays strong, then buying foreign currency in the forward market may be more expensive than it need have been. But living with uncertainty can itself be costly. Using forward markets means that the business has agreed a price and it will not change.

If Majestic had bought the euros right away in the forward market, before the pound depreciated, it would have saved a lot of money. Having done so, Majestic would have some flexibility as to the prices it charged. It could keep the old price and advertise no change, or it could charge more and enjoy a higher profit margin.

> **Forward markets** make it possible to buy foreign currencies at a price agreed today, for delivery on a specific future date. This can be seen as insurance against an unfavourable change in the exchange rate that might affect profitability. It is also possible to buy commodities and financial assets in forward markets. These contracts made in forward markets are called futures.

The role of insurance

Spreading risks

When we insure against a certain type of risk, a premium is paid. In return for this payment, the insurance company promises to compensate the insured person or business, if the event actually happens. Insurance is a way of spreading risks by sharing their cost. It protects the insured from some of the consequences of unforeseen events.

The premium covers both the cost of compensating the insured when things go wrong and the administrative cost to the insurance company of offering the service. It isn't hard to see why the terms and conditions may be quite restrictive. The insurance company has to have reserves to cover all likely claims, plus enough income to pay its employees and the rent on its office space. The terms and conditions therefore spell out exactly what kind of liability the insurance company is taking on. Anything excluded in the contract will mean that a customer's claim will be denied or limited.

Individuals and businesses choose what they want to insure.

Example
By law, your car must have third party insurance, so that if you knock someone down, there is enough money to compensate them or their relatives for the consequences of your action. If you have an old car you might save some money by insuring the car for just third party, fire and theft. This might make sense. If the car is not worth much, your losses if it gets written off will not be very serious if. If you have a new car, you would be foolish not to have comprehensive insurance.

Businesses need many kinds of insurance: buildings and equipment, vehicles, ships and aircraft are obvious. They also need public liability insurance.

Public liability insurance

Example
Most businesses need some public liability insurance in case someone from outside the business gets injured or disadvantaged as a result of their activities. Then by law they must have employers' liability insurance in case an employee gets hurt while working. People who give advice need professional indemnity insurance in case they are sued for giving bad advice.

There is always a choice about how much insurance is needed. The higher the sum insured, the bigger the premium. Insurance can be costly so some people may try to keep it to a minimum. However, if you think

Minimising risk

about travelling abroad without health insurance, you might change your mind when something goes badly wrong.

From the business point of view, being adequately insured may make the difference between survival and closing down. Equally, it is an overhead cost that must be considered when deciding on pricing strategies. It makes excellent sense to share the risks of major losses through insurance, even though for a small business the costs may seem very high. Some businesses may be tempted to carry their own insurance (i.e. take out only the legally required insurance policies). This makes sense only if they know they have adequate reserves to cover all eventualities. That would be alright for Apple, with its $40 billion of retained profits, but not for many other businesses. It is not alright for people whose work takes them up ladders.

Find out

The Money Super Market website has a Business Insurance Guide. Spend just a few minutes looking at the range of insurance options.

Show your understanding

In 2016, H&M suffered as the US dollar strengthened. The Swedish clothing retailer buys most of its goods in Asia under a dollar-denominated purchasing deal. As the dollar appreciated, H&M's costs rose. On top of that, sales were down because of the cold spring in Europe. In its biggest market, Germany, sales were flat through the six months to the end of May. But the CEO was still optimistic. He said "*The combination of strong brands, a large body of retail stores in good locations and a successful ecommerce business puts us in a unique market position for future growth.*" The company operates over 4,000 stores in 62 countries; in the same period, sales grew by 7% in the US.

1. Explain how H&M could have avoided the rising costs.

2. Other clothing retailers, such as the Irish company Primark, are opening new sales outlets in the USA too. Explain why the CEO may have been overly optimistic.

3. Examine the pros and cons of the H&M strategy.

Chapter 17
The role of the financial sector

Terms to revise: the role of banks in the economy, sources of finance, working capital, (all in Theme 1).

Banking

Banks take deposits from savers and lend money to investors. Banking seems to have started about 4,000 years ago in Mesopotamia. Those banks had two functions: to safeguard treasure for those who acquired it and to fund trade between different locations. The ancient Greeks and Romans had banks too. Later, in northern Europe, from around 1300 onwards, people in England began borrowing from bankers located in northern Italy. We know that monasteries in the UK west country were borrowing then in order to expand their sheep farming operations. English wool fetched good prices in Antwerp.

Banking was often very risky. When the price of wool fell, some of the monasteries were unable to repay their loans and the bank in Florence went bankrupt too.

Discussion points

Why would banks lend to risky businesses?

How does lending help the borrowers?

How does borrowing and lending help the economy?

Ancient banks made money by lending, just as banks do now. Interest payments made them rich. Much later, the banks realised that their depositors would not all want to withdraw their assets at once. This allowed the banks to lend more than the sum total of their deposits, guaranteeing their debts with notes. These gradually evolved into today's bank notes. Lending in this way is called **credit creation**; it has been immensely important in helping economies to grow.

Credit creation

Money and the finance sector

It helps to start by looking at what money can do. It is:

● a medium of exchange – we use it to buy and sell goods and services.

● a way to measure value, showing the relative value of different things.

● a store of value – it is an asset that can be saved rather than spent now.

● a way to spread payments over a period of time (deferred payment).

Financial intermediaries are organisations that channel funds generated by savers towards borrowers who want to spend or invest. Storing value means saving money for later – in a risky world it makes sense to have reserves. Deferring payments is what we do when we borrow to buy something big – a new car, a home, production equipment, a factory or office building.

> **Credit creation** is the process by which banks expand their lending by a multiple of the deposits they receive. There are risks involved. So it is vitally important that banks assess the risks associated with their lending and do not expand their lending activity beyond safe limits.
>
> **Financial intermediaries** include all organisations that take savers' funds and lend to investors. They include banks, building societies, pension funds and insurance companies.

Facilitating the exchange of goods and services

Money as a *medium of exchange* facilitates the buying and selling of goods and services. Money makes this easy: the alternative is barter, i.e. swapping one good or service for another. To become better off, we have to specialise, which makes us more efficient. Money facilitates specialisation and the process of economic growth.

Exchange

> **Example**
> It took many highly educated people to design and create your iPhone. These people cannot grow their own food and make their own clothes as well. So they must have money. Money and exchange enhance specialisation because they give us a simple way to get more of what we need and want. We benefit from the expertise of very specialised people with scarce skills.

Banks have created payment mechanisms that enable the exchange of goods and services. In the past, cash and cheque books worked well. Later, credit and debit cards and bank transfers cut the costs of transactions, leading to further efficiency improvements. They all took off very quickly – because they saved almost everyone time and money. Banks play a big part in foreign exchange payments, facilitating international trade.

Lending savings and borrowing to spend or invest

Security

Banks give individuals a secure place for money saved until they face an emergency or are ready to spend it. Depositors provide banks with funds to lend to individuals and businesses. Banks make money by charging a higher rate of interest to borrowers and giving a lower rate on savings. The difference pays for banking services and the costs of carrying risks.

The interaction of savers and borrowers creates market forces. If many people want to borrow but few want to save, funds will be scarce. This will push up interest rates. But it will also provide more of an incentive for savers, increasing the flow of funds.

Banks can carry risks much more safely than individual savers. The risks can be spread across a wide range of borrowers; only a few will default on their debts. Banks have a wealth of experience in carefully assessing the risk of lending to potential borrowers.

Working capital

Retail banks offer banking services to individuals and businesses. These services include current and savings accounts, mortgages, foreign exchange deals and some kinds of insurance. They are important providers of loans and overdrafts for businesses that need working capital to cover their costs until sales revenue comes in. (For many businesses this can take up to 60 days.) This is particularly important for exporters. They also lend to individuals with good credit ratings.

> **Find out**
> …what services your bank offers.

Investment banks mostly serve bigger businesses. They specialise in lending for big projects. For something really big like the Channel Tunnel, investment banks will form a consortium, working together. They have a significant role in M&A (mergers and acquisitions) and selling new share issues including IPOs (initial public offerings, launched by private companies that are just about to go public). The best-known investment bank is Goldman Sachs.

Investment banks also trade in foreign currencies, commodities, bonds and derivatives. *Bonds* are loans issued by both businesses and governments. They are usually for a fixed term, maybe one year or more, and they can be sold in the event of their owner needing the money immediately. *Derivatives* are financial products that are related to underlying bundles of assets such as commodities, currencies or shares and are priced accordingly. Many derivatives are linked to purchases in forward markets.

Building societies offer mortgages for house purchase and lend only the savings that people have deposited with them. They do not create credit, as banks do. They have a reputation for safety. Many have offered savers better interest rates than the banks typically do. They have the expertise to assess borrowers' credit-worthiness, just as banks do.

Pension funds and **insurance companies** accumulate large sums through pension schemes and sales of insurance policies. These funds must be kept for a time when payments must be made. So both are big investors. They buy significant quantities of equities (shares in plcs) and bonds issued by both businesses and governments (including local authorities). As shareholders they have considerable influence over big plcs. They are sometimes referred to as institutional shareholders.

Other financial intermediaries have developed recently and include **crowdfunding platforms** and **peer-to-peer** lenders. These develop on-line communities of potential lenders. They are usually riskier than the financial intermediaries listed above. Lenders can spread the risks somewhat by making sure that they do not invest too much in any one business.

Shadow banking

Shadow banking refers to financial intermediaries that are not banks but borrow and lend in similar ways. Banks are tightly regulated so as to prevent financial crises and reduce risks for customers. Shadow banks can stay outside the regulatory system. There is real concern that shadow banking could trigger a new financial crisis. The IMF says:

> *"Shadow banks borrow short-term funds in the money markets and use those funds to buy assets with longer-term maturities. But because they are not subject to traditional bank regulation, they cannot – as banks can – borrow in an emergency from their central bank."*

Assessing creditor risk

Most of us are aware of credit ratings. There are agencies that specialise in finding out about past debts. Someone who fails to pay their mortgage or credit card bills will be identified and put on a list. Owners of businesses that have become insolvent will be recorded as potential credit risks. If you always pay your bills on time you will have a good credit rating.

Getting a bank loan involves giving a lot of information about previous financial activity and any existing loans. Banks and building societies protect their savers' interests by maintaining their own reliability and that means assessing the riskiness of the loans and mortgages they plan to provide. Credit assessments also take account of job prospects and income levels.

Collateral

Risk assessment for businesses involves careful scrutiny of the accounts. Where the risk is considered too great, borrowing may still be possible if there is collateral. For small businesses that have not been trading for long collateral will often be the owner's house. It can greatly increase the risks carried by the borrower but protects the lender.

If you always pay your bills on time you will have a good credit rating.

Financial markets

If many businesses want to borrow in order to invest, interest rates will rise. However, some projects will still be viable – higher interest rates will simply force investors to consider which projects can be funded and which not. Also, with more incentives for savers, funding for investment may increase. In turn, this helps investors to develop activities that benefit society. Efficient financial markets help to create prosperous economies. Banks hold deposits safely and finance business expansion.